"The challenge of training godly children in an ungodly environment is not essentially different than it was during the New Testament era or during most of the Old Testament era. The so-called elite movers and shakers of the world have always promoted a worldview that defies God. What is different today is that the media and secular public education along with the weakening of family structures and a lessening of family time together have intensified the bombardment of Christian children with ungodly influences. This book provides guidance for pastors, teachers, and parents to help them understand and counter the forces that are trying to pull their children away from God. It does not offer quick-fix solutions but provides help for designing and implementing a battle plan in this struggle. This is a challenging book to confront a challenging problem."

—Dr. John F. Brug
The Wartburg Project

"The challenge to faithfully follow Christ in the midst of a fallen and hostile world is not new, but in the West after Christendom, it is often not only demanding but also frustrating, bewildering, and discouraging. Using a wealth of scriptural narratives and encouragement, Kremer exhorts his reader to greet this challenge not with trepidation or resignation, but with conviction, resolution, and even confident joy. Such purposeful Christian living is essential, because, as the author rightly insists, the stakes are extraordinarily, indeed, eternally high."

—Dr. Joel Biermann
Professor of Systematic Theology
Concordia Seminary, St. Louis, MO

"Kenn Kremer writes a compelling call to action for Christians concerned about reflecting godly character in an increasingly secular and godless culture. He explains how biblical truths, both Law and Gospel, apply to Christians today. He contrasts a secular, godless worldview that emphasizes material worth and self-glorification with a Christian worldview that emphasizes eternal truths and glorification of the triune God rather than self. The book and discussion guide are valuable resources for Christians, especially pastors, teachers, leaders, and support God's children in the development of godly characteristics in an ungodly culture."

—Dr. Carla Melendy
Professor Emeritus
Martin Luther College, New Ulm, MN

"Kenneth Kremer's *Embracing Godly Character: The Christian Community's Response to a Godless Culture* surveys the cultural confusion swirling all around today's Christian family, and, from the high ground of Scripture, points us back to joy, peace, and blessings founded in God's promises. Kremer's broad review includes a useful chapter-by-chapter discussion guide to help us approach many practicalities of living in a godly way. And don't miss the short, topical Bible studies embedded in footnotes; these are hidden gems! All in all, this book provides a bracing reality check and a thought-provoking strategic perspective. I like this book!"

—Dr. Jesse Yow
Author of *Standing Firm: A Christian Response to Hostility and Persecution*

"*Embracing Godly Character* is an enjoyable read. Kenn uses an interesting blend of history, God's Word, and a Lutheran lens to put our modern cultural dilemmas into context. He provides excellent insights for both individuals and family leaders about how to combat modern culture's negative influence on spiritual character, and he does it in a very readable format. Thanks, Kenn, for giving voice to what many Christians have sensed but not been able to clearly articulate."

—Dr. John Meyer
Director of Graduate Studies
Martin Luther College, New Ulm, MN

"This well-written book speaks sharply to our turbulent times and calls us from complacency about the surrounding culture. Kremer urges us to focus on our family life. Firmly based on Scripture, he shows how Christian character and worldview are developed. Kremer skillfully distinguishes the place of personal identity as primary and how in the Christian alone this finds true synthesis with how we should act. This book can be a very useful tool for discussion in a church study group. Young parents setting the tone in their homes will especially benefit. All who are concerned for the children of the Church will feel a renewed spirit."

—Dr. Paul R. Boehlke

Professor Emeritus of Biology, Wisconsin Lutheran College, Milwaukee, WI
Adjunct Instructor, Graduate Studies, Martin Luther College, New Ulm, MN

"'God is my refuge and strength. . . .' These words have been recited by Christians worldwide for thousands of years through times of great distress. We live in such times. Opposition to Christianity now works to intimidate God's people into silence. Kenn Kremer's book reminds us that the Gospel is timeless, that biblical teaching is the source of all true knowledge, and is still 'an ever-present help in trouble.' This book points to the dangers, new and old, that we must endure on our pathway to our heavenly home. It is an invaluable reminder and encouragement for the Christian parent, minister, teacher, employee, and public servant."

—Rep. Jeremy Thiesfeldt
WI State Assembly—52nd District

"Jesus tells His followers that although we are *in* the world, we are not *of* the world. How, then, shall we live—especially as we find ourselves in an increasingly godless and Christ-less culture? Kenneth Kremer takes up the challenge, enlisting a wide range of historical and contemporary sources along with years of personal experience in the teaching and writing ministries. Above all, he draws deeply from the most reliable source of guidance, the Holy Scriptures. *Embracing Godly Character* focuses on Christian homes, but individuals and church groups will also find this an excellent guide to living for our Savior."

—Dr. Roland Cap Ehlke

Professor of Philosophy at Concordia University Wisconsin, Mequon, WI
Author of *Like a Pelting Rain: The Making of the Modern Mind*

Embracing Godly Character

The Christian Community's Response to a Godless Culture

Kenneth Kremer

Published by Concordia Publishing House
3558 S. Jefferson Ave., St. Louis, MO 63118–3968
1-800-325-3040 • cph.org

Manufactured in the United States of America

Library of Congress Cataloging-in-Publication Data

Names: Kremer, Kenneth, author.

Title: Embracing godly character : the Christian community's response to a godless culture / by Kenneth J. Kremer.

Description: St. Louis, MO : Concordia Publishing House, [2018] | Includes bibliographical references.

Identifiers: LCCN 2017048931 (print) | LCCN 2017059407 (ebook) | ISBN 9780758659880 | ISBN 9780758659873

Subjects: LCSH: Character--Religious aspects--Christianity. | Character--Biblical teaching. | Christianity and culture.

Classification: LCC BV4599.5.C45 (ebook) | LCC BV4599.5.C45 K74 2018 (print) | DDC 261--dc23

LC record available at https://lccn.loc.gov/2017048931

1 2 3 4 5 6 7 8 9 10 27 26 25 24 23 22 21 20 19 18

In loving memory of my dear mother,
Lydia C. Kremer,
1921–2016

Table of Contents

Foreword

One of the most important Irish-Anglo statesmen of Western Civilization was Edmund Burke. He also penned the most famous antirevolutionary book ever written, warning that revolution in France would end up with violence and bloodshed in the streets. Burke was prophetic; the revolution failed, and the great man's insight has come to be seen as a glory and a roadmap after the tragedy of Paris.

Burke showed that any country, culture, or civilization that does not place virtue at the center of what it means to be a good citizen—and especially among the young—is a country, culture, and civilization that is hollow and doomed. Burke's greatest insight was that morals and manners mattered more than laws and statutes.

Kenneth Kremer has written a truly wonderful and even profound book. He aims not to whistle down the wind of our chaotic climate but rather to float an elemental idea that has power. He says that if moms and dads want to raise great kids, they ought to pay attention—from first to last—to their children's character; their moral architecture; their manners. He shows why habituating integrity from the youngest of ages is a powerful antidote to the cultural tsunami in which we find ourselves awash.

Yet the mastery of his prose and the generosity of his soul is not a point-by-point analysis of what needs to be done to raise a great generation of young people. Instead, he points to the holy cross of mercy and grace and says that the way forward for Christians in this troubled era is to preoccupy ourselves with influencing, shaping, and molding godly character. What a refreshing and nourishing prospect.

But how does one embrace such a character, and what does it mean to be godly? The book unfolds like a soft Irish rain: no knuckles in the chest. No gloom and doom. No major warnings. Instead, Kremer restates the first principles of the Christian life and finds a tender manner and idiom of reintroducing those principles for this new and sometimes brutal and asymmetrical era.

A great president of the United States once posited that "There is no better way to establish hope for the future than to enlighten young minds." Kremer is keen to enlighten young hearts and souls too. His end point is a grace note and a very fine read.

Tim Goeglein

Tim Goeglein is Vice President for External Relations at Focus on the Family and a Senior Fellow at The Heritage Foundation in Washington, DC. He served in high-level government posts for the past two decades. He worked as Special Assistant to President George W. Bush, where he was the Deputy Director of the White House Office of Public Liaison from 2001 to 2008. Goeglein is the author of the political memoir *The Man in the Middle: An Inside Account of Faith and Politics in the George W. Bush Era.*

Acknowledgments

As I look back four years to the beginning of this project, I realize now that it never could have happened without the help and encouragement of a small army. Ryan Olson, for example, suggested I read James Davison Hunter, Joel Biermann, Charles Taylor, James K. A. Smith, and Jean-Jacques Rousseau. These writers and thinkers provided a philosophical framework. Philip Koelpin insisted I reread Siegbert Becker's classic *The Foolishness of God* and C. F. W. Walther's timeless *God's No and God's Yes*. Their contributions became the theological and historical foundation. Matthew Hoehner suggested I take a look at *The Genius of Luther's Theology* by Robert Kolb and Charles Arand. The view was breathtaking. Paul Boehlke encouraged me to read Martin Galstad's *Findings*—simply profound. Roland Cap Ehlke encouraged me to take a look at *The Law above the Law* by John Warwick Montgomery—a brilliant work. Thank you to all who contributed to the project's literary and biblical perspective.

I was also blessed with some of the best critics anyone could want, including my graduate students at Martin Luther College in New Ulm, Minnesota, a district conference that met in 2015 in Findlay, Ohio, and a cadre of ministry associates in the Appleton area. The thoughtful readings of portions of the manuscript by the following individuals helped guide the project's progress: Carla Melendy, Paul Boehlke, Ronald Gorske, James Westendorf, Mark and Molly Parsons, Adam Zimplemann, Andrea Vinji, John Roekle, Kenneth Kratz, John Juern, James Pope, Jonathan Kuske, Thomas Mielke, John Miller, William Monday, Benjamin Burger, and Jonathan Ruddat. Kati Guenterberg and Rosie Bunnow edited sections of the manuscript. Bless you all for your generosity and willingness to help.

I am especially indebted to Roland Cap Ehlke for his edit of the original manuscript. Cap, your insights gave me a clear path to completing the project. I also want to acknowledge the wonderful people at CPH. In particular, a special thank you goes out to Laura Lane, Joe Willmann, and Peter Jurchen. I will always cherish your friendship and the professional commitment you made to this project.

Finally, I daily thank God for the loving support and selfless patience of my dear wife, Marlis. The countless hours we spent together discussing culture, worldviews, and her discerning thoughts about the formation of biblical character were truly priceless. I am even more grateful for making me her own special project in life. Bless you, Dear Heart. *—KJK*

Introduction

It should not shock us anymore to hear that we live in a godless culture. Historians are calling it the Post-Christian Era. Of course, this doesn't mean that God has abandoned us. It means that a lot of people have abandoned Him in favor of the many godless "isms" that flourish in society today—materialism, humanism, existentialism, secularism, pluralism, Spiritism, atheism, and others. For a growing number of Americans, the Bible seems quaint—a literary relic. Some even think of Christianity as being countercultural.

In spite of secular philosophies and profane worldviews, God is still speaking to us. The inspired words of Scripture are His. His Law still demands holiness. His essential message is still life and light. The Gospel comforts, encourages, gives hope to fallen mankind. It saves. God is not dead. He is alive forever. He has not moved to an undisclosed location. He is with us and blesses us, as He has promised. Knowing this is important, because the unbelieving world would like us to think that the message of salvation in Christ is falling on deaf ears.

The discussion that follows is unapologetic about its headwaters for truth. God's Word is our stronghold—our anchor in a riotous sea of change. We trust it to be as relevant today as it was in any other season of our world's history. If we are to understand what godly character is, how it is formed, or why the interaction between character and culture is so important, we will want God's Word shedding its light on our conversation.

For anyone looking for a prophetic view of where our culture is headed, this book isn't for you. It may also disappoint some to learn this book is not a rant about the decline of Western civilization, the fall of democracy, or the demise of capitalism. It does not represent a call for expanding alternate educational models—homeschooling, online education, and the like. While we have the utmost respect for good science and empirical data, the case being made is not of human origin; it is informed by the impeccable truth of divinely inspired Scripture and not by statistical evidence. Nor will politics have a voice. Our intent is to hold the higher ground of God's inspired Word, where spirit and truth are golden and the miracle of salvation is the pearl of supreme worth. We will not, per se, be discussing the Bible's position regarding specific sins and godless lifestyles—materialism and greed, the LGBTQ movement, urban violence, pornography, abortion, human slavery, turning a blind eye to hunger and poverty, racial and ethnic tensions, euthanasia, and so on. These conversations are desperately needed among God's people, but each is deserving of a separate study. We have also resisted the urge to turn the clock back to a romanticized version of the past. We will, however, pay our respects to history every now and then, to gain insights regarding causes and effects. We will make a serious effort to understand the complex, confusing, and ever-changing present age. And we will discuss what makes people distinctively human without injecting the mandatory conversations about the ego, the id, or personality types.

In the final analysis, this book's main thrust will center on the Christian community's response to a culture that is becoming increasingly unsympathetic to believers. More than anything, this is a book about priming the pump for an overdue conversation about raising a godly family in a culture that is, at its core, secular. The book's message, then, is intended first for parents.

In the Bible, parents are understood as God's frontline warriors. They are the vanguard for shaping the next generation's moral views. Parenting is a vocational calling of unselfish leadership and humble, personal ministry. For those readers who do not like to be overwhelmed with details, this book's main body offers a quick, easy read that builds a case for encouraging Christian fathers and mothers to commit themselves to a more robust exercise of their family's faith life at home. Discussion questions have been added to stimulate productive conversations among parents (see *Appendix A: Discussion Guide*).

There is also an urgent need to generate a lively conversation among leaders of the organized church—pastors, ministry teams, lay ministers, and Christian educators—about spiritual life in the privacy of our homes. Change doesn't happen without a firm commitment from called church leaders. Members rely on their leaders, especially their pastors, to provide guidance in developing ministry plans, constructing program elements, setting aside budgetary resources, and making sure their church's ministry plan is being implemented. Appended study aids have been included in the book to assist in developing some of the more pressing discussion topics. A free set of thought-provoking discussion points entitled "Conversation Starters for Church Leaders" is available at the Steeples website: embracingchristiancharacter.com.

In a culture ever morphing and constantly mutating, we need to assess the damage that our changing culture has done to the Christian family over the last half century. In the following pages, we will consider the who, what, when, where, and how of character formation. We will talk about the influence that our changing culture has had on character. We will address questions about moral authority and examine aspects of biblical character that have been forgotten, ignored, or hijacked by popular norms. With a humble and prayerful heart, we will discuss strategies for reaching inward with the Gospel to the members of our own families and outward with that same Good News to a world languishing in unbelief.

This is a conversation that cannot be dismissed. To be frank, it is not without risk or peril. We all struggle to become the kind of people God intended us to be.

Yet, we fail frequently and are often disappointed in the behaviors of our fellow Christians. As you approach these chapters, come with a Bible in your hand and a prayer on your lips. Then relax. As God's Word has promised, "Do not be anxious about anything, but in everything by prayer and supplication with thanksgiving let your requests be made known to God. And the peace of God, which surpasses all understanding, will guard your hearts and your minds in Christ Jesus" (Philippians 4:6–7).

A Parable

There once lived a Christian man, who loved his wife and children deeply. In the spring of their lives, the man worked very hard to provide for his family. He made every effort to be a loyal companion to his wife and an exemplary father to his children. In time, he saved enough money to build a beautiful, new house—a haven, safe from wild animals and shielded from noisy neighbors. Many other people settled in the same green valley. The opportunities for making new friends, attending new schools, exploring new shopping centers, and finding new jobs increased quickly.

As the valley's population grew, the man's children gathered new ideas from the melting pot of cultural backgrounds. They rubbed elbows every day with them. The man's children seemed to thrive on the freedom to shape their own identity without boundaries or restraints of any kind. The man thought, This is good. Now my children can truly become their own persons and create their own destinies in life.

As the leaves turned from green to orange, the man noticed a draft wafting through the hallways of his new house. This will never do, he thought. Winter will soon be upon us. If I do not insulate my house against the cold, we will freeze. So, the man weather-stripped all the doors and windows and put a thick layer of insulation in the attic.

Soon the gales of November whistled in from the north, but the house still was not airtight. The cold crept in beneath the floorboards and through the tiny cracks by the windowsills. No one complained. In fact, they hardly noticed the cold because the family's collective hearts were being warmed by a new kind of sharing. The man's family had become connected with all the other people on the globe by a magic device. This, too, hastened the day when each child would become his or her own person.

The man's family seemed happy, but the man was troubled. With each passing day, he felt more alone. He also saw that his children talked less with one another or their father and mother. He wondered what good a family was if its members stopped laughing together and working together. He noticed that the neighbors didn't seem as neighborly either. People moved in and out of their homes quickly. No one could keep up with the changing names and faces living on their block. Even the local church seemed to be in distress. Church members began to distance themselves from one another, until many of them forgot why they had belonged to a church in the first place.

Finally, the man instructed his family to come together in a room every day to talk and live like a family. But by this time, each child had become his or her own person, so the room they were all told to gather in remained empty and cold.

The December blizzards came, and the man's family huddled under piles of blankets, shivering. In desperation, the man hired experts to add new layers of high-tech, pink insulation around the outside walls of the house. Experts would know just how thick the insulation had to be. New technologies were being invented all the time—one to deal with inclement weather, another to fight illness, one to escape gravity's pull, and one to make crops produce more food. If people didn't have the appropriate technology to overcome a certain problem, they would invent one.

The days of raging blizzards soon turned into weeks of subzero temperatures. The man was beside himself to find a solution to the bitter cold outside. Sometimes, he wondered how he might have built his home differently.

Then one brutally cold January morning, the man awoke to find himself alone. A note on the kitchen table explained, "We've gone to look for a home with a warm fire burning in the hearth."

Jesus answered him, "Truly, truly, I say to you,
unless one is born again he
cannot see the kingdom of God."

—John 3:3

CHAPTER 1

High-Level Conversations

In biblical times, the formation of godly character often involved conversations that occurred in unusual circumstances. Abraham, for example, found his identity on a mountaintop, with a knife in his hand and his son Isaac laid out before him like a sacrificial lamb (see Genesis 22:1–14). When God provided a ram that would be accepted as Isaac's substitute, Abraham gratefully named that mountain "The Lord will provide" (Genesis 22:14). Queen Esther's moment of truth happened as she calmly stood before the throne of her husband-king, who had the power to execute her for entering his throne room without an invitation. God had placed Esther into this dangerous position and given her the courage to stand firm in the face of death in order to preserve the ancestral line for the promised Messiah. That bloodline needed to remain intact to fulfill God's prophecies concerning His eternal plan to save humankind from sin's curse (Esther 4–5). Elijah discovered his identity when he finally understood God's identity. It happened when he heard the gentle, whispered voice of his almighty God's infinite love (1 Kings 19). Jonah discovered who he was from inside the belly of a giant fish (Jonah 1).

One of the most captivating character meetings of all time was also one of the Bible's briefest conversations. It took place on a rocky outcropping outside Jerusalem's walls. The Romans used the site to execute criminals. On this day, the city was shrouded in an eerie pall of darkness. Three men were being crucified. The character of the man hanging on the center cross was as pure and innocent as the driven snow. Yet, He had been tried and found guilty by a corrupt Sanhedrin that heard false testimony and brought bogus charges against Him. The final orders for His execution had come at the hands of the Roman governor of Judea, Pontius Pilate.

The name of the man hanging on that center cross was Jesus. The name means "The LORD Is Our Salvation." His countenance was darker than the skies over Jerusalem. He was carrying the guilt of the entire human race to His death. This dying Jesus was God's sacrificial offering—the Lamb of God—His only Son.

The Romans had spiked Jesus' hands and feet to a makeshift cross. There, He would hang, suspended between heaven and earth for six agonizing hours, finally offering Himself up in death as the full ransom to buy back His rebellious creatures from sin's curse.

The hearts of the men being crucified on either side of Jesus were also cloaked in darkness. One felon was so stonyhearted from evil influences that all he could do was curse the Romans and demean Jesus for thinking He was some kind of king.

The other fellow's heart was darkened more by his haunting memories of the depraved life he had lived. It was clear, even to himself, that he was not a good man. Though we don't know for sure, one can imagine how he could not remember doing one decent thing for anyone. It's likely that he felt just as guilty about the good he had never done as he did about the awful things he had done.

Who could love a person like that? Yet, Jesus seemed to take an interest in this man's parting agony.

The thief wished his life might still be acknowledged by someone. Perhaps he wondered what harm there would be in sharing a final thought—a prayer, of sorts—addressed to the man at the center of everyone's attention. "Jesus," he said, "remember me when You come into Your kingdom" (Luke 23:42).

It didn't take long for the man to get a response. "Truly, I say to you," replied Jesus, "today you will be with Me in paradise" (v. 43). End of conversation.

We can only guess how the thief tried to grasp the implications of what he had just heard. Could he have wondered what he might have said or done to deserve such a grand promise? We can speculate that he had begun the conversation with the hope that his life might still be given some significance. Being remembered by the Son of God would have arisen far above such hope. In the blink of an eye, everything changed. Death was now the man's passage to immortality. New life was in his grasp. His tortured final moments were bathed in light and filled with joy. The man knew Jesus. He knew Jesus' heart, His forgiveness, His holy love. What irony! With only hours remaining, the man had suddenly received purpose and meaning for a life that only minutes earlier had been completely worthless. He had come to identify himself with the dying man on the center cross. Jesus was his Savior, his Lord of life. With whatever time was left, we assume he would have quietly glorified his Lord Jesus in the privacy of his heart. Soon, his everlasting future would be spent in the eternal kingdom paradise that Jesus had been referring to, joyfully doing the same.

These are, of course, not the only lives God has touched. Our conversation will embrace other changes of the heart that are just as miraculous, including yours and mine.

When it comes to character, change is a great place to begin. The formation of godly character always involves change that is radical, ongoing, and compelling. Change is one of the dynamics that will drive our conversation.

DEFINING CHARACTER

Coming to a clear understanding of my "self" is a lifelong learning curve. As a critical element in the shaping of character, learning is one of the most important kinds of change any human being can experience. The prolific author and lecturer Stanley Hauerwas, a champion of the virtue-ethics movement of the 1980s and '90s, famously writes, "Ethics is never finally a matter of theory; rather, it is a reflective activity not easily learned."[1] The forming of human character is actually a lifetime learning process. What we are becoming depends largely on a combination of human experiences and influences. But the Bible tells us there is more to the story of our moral formation. Scripture says that every human being is born with a sense of what is moral and what is not, and this innate sense rests in what believers understand as a divine ethic.[2] So, in moral terms, we do not arrive in this life with a blank slate.

Dwight L. Moody (1837–99), a popular theologian in the latter half of the nineteenth century, exposed a disturbing aspect of human character. Moody said, "Character is what you are in the dark."[3] His definition implies the presence of sin in every human heart. He is suggesting that character is who I am, warts and all. Moody was right. We must all learn the truth about our evil desires and inclinations. We must know, too, the dreadful consequences for sin, the shame connected with sin, and the hopeless damage our own immoral living has done to destroy our relationship with our righteous and loving God.

Our sinful behavior has not only destroyed our relationship with God, but it also has the potential to ruin our relationships with family members, friends,

1 Stanley Hauerwas, *The Peaceable Kingdom: A Primer in Christian Ethics* (Notre Dame, IN: University of Notre Dame Press, 1983), xv.

2 See Romans 2:14–15.

3 Suzy Platt, ed., *Respectfully Quoted: A Dictionary of Quotations* (New York: Barnes and Noble Books, 1993), § 187, p. 40: Attributed to Dwight L. Moody by his son, William R. Moody, in *D. L. Moody*, p. 503 (1930).

The image others see when they are faced with someone of truly Christian character is Christ.

colleagues, and neighbors. Knowing this, we quickly learn to hide our most repulsive thoughts and behaviors from others, often with sneaky deception. We know, only too well, that the nasty truth about how we conduct our lives undermines the trust others have placed in us. For this reason, every child instinctively knows what it is to tell a lie.

Godly character begins with integrity.[4] Any honest study of character must account for the masks we wear to conceal our moral flaws. But in that same discussion, we will also note the biblical truth that our masks of disgrace are transformed by faith in Jesus. The image others see when they are faced with someone of truly Christian character is Christ. To say that in a slightly different way, godly men, women, and children are the masks God wears when He wants to project His goodness and love to His own people and the unbelieving world.

A revolutionary thinker of his day, the French philosopher Jean-Jacques Rousseau (1712–78) was an early advocate for letting character gel on its own. In an era when educational models were very different from contemporary learning models, Rousseau opposed public education, favoring a more natural path. Rousseau assumed that children can find their own way in life if they merely recognize that, as equals to all others, their calling is to be a decent human being. The following quote from Rousseau's book *Emile* or *On Education* gives us a sense of his worldview regarding the formation of character and explains why Rousseau's writings still influence our culture today.

> Our true study is that of the human condition. He among us who best knows how to bear the goods and the ills of this life is to my taste the best raised: from which it follows that the true education consists less in precept than in practice. We begin to instruct ourselves when we begin to live. Our education begins with us.[5]

Rousseau's entire focus was on serving the needs of this life. He was most concerned about satisfying the needs of the self. Rousseau's worldview reflects a human perspective. It is secular and bears all the marks of humanism before it was fashionable. And many of Rousseau's ideas are embedded in our nation's founding principles. His understanding of what constitutes a decent human being is not biblical, though it is understandable from a human standpoint. While unbelievers

4 See *Appendix B: Biblical Character*.

5 Jean-Jacques Rousseau, *Emile* or *On Education*, trans. Allan Bloom (New York: Basic Books, 1979), 41–42.

insist that every human being should "know thyself," God's Word makes it clear that our highest priority in life is to know *God* and His love for us.

Speaking about knowledge and the role education plays in building character, Herbert Spencer (1820–1903) declared,

> Education has for its object the formation of character. To curb restive propensities, to awaken dormant sentiments, to strengthen the perceptions and cultivate the tastes, to encourage this feeling and repress that, so as finally to develop the child into a man of well proportioned and harmonious nature—this is alike the aim of parent and teacher.[6]

Today, in an age of early education, powerful delivery systems for every subject, and individualized learning strategies, character building should engage parents and teachers in a common cause. But Spencer wrote these words before the American Civil War. He believed that the only meaningful philosophical problems are those that can be solved by logical analysis. God's Word doesn't always line up with the logical analysis of human thought.[7] Rational human logic has little tolerance for angels, a heavenly kingdom, miracles, prayer, a physical resurrection, or a belief system that rests on the notion of God's boundless grace. Spencer wasn't speaking about the kind of character Christian parents want for their children. He was proposing a kind of character that would fit the needs of an enlightened society that was eager to replace biblical truth with secular ideas that would make life in the here and now more tolerable. To accomplish this, it was necessary to invent the diabolical myth that human beings are inherently good. Where that lie serves as the foundation for a conversation about ethics, God's people need to talk about character and its formation in an environment enlightened by biblical truth.

A CONVERSATION ABOUT MORALITY

In recent decades, much of the serious talk about character has gone underground. It doesn't help that the popular culture surrounds us with messages that promote self-image, self-confidence, self-improvement, and self-importance. Today, character is defined as "innate," and it is framed as a system of self-generated values. *Innate* means we are born with it. When challenged, some will even excuse their behavior, saying, "This is the way God made me." To say it is "self-generated"

---

6 Platt, *Respectfully Quoted*, § 501, p. 99. Quoted from *Social Statics* (1851) by Herbert Spencer, p. 180. An English academic, Spencer (1820–1903) contributed to studies in ethics, religion, anthropology, economics, political theory, and philosophy.

7 See Isaiah 55:8.

This notion of leaving character formation up to the individual leaves little room for the biblical concept that we are shaped by the virtues and values that others pass on to us.

suggests we develop our moral code as we go, according to our own whims and fancies. When character is defined in this way, its formation relies on personal choices to determine whatever ethical materials will be used for constructing one's own moral compass. The burden of formation in the model that Rousseau and Spencer advocated rests almost entirely on the sin-saturated self. This approach says, "My character is all about me—my desires, my worldviews, my will." But this is just not how character works. This notion of leaving character formation up to the individual leaves little room for the biblical concept that we are shaped by the virtues and values that others pass on to us. David Brooks, the popular columnist, writes:

> No person can achieve self-mastery on his own or her own. Individual will, reason, compassion and character are not strong enough to consistently defeat selfishness, pride, greed, and self-deception. Everybody needs redemptive assistance from outside—from family, friends, ancestors, rules, traditions, institutions, exemplars, and, for believers, God.[8]

There is a new understanding of character today that, for Christians, has disturbing overtones. When character is understood as innate morality or self-generated codes, it is easy for sinful people to replace godly humility with swagger and by-our-own-bootstraps self-redemption. Without social constraint, self-gratification and immodesty can easily trump chastity and purity. Without communal input, revenge can be justified, and living in peace with one's neighbors can be redefined as optional. When integrity is not reinforced as a virtue, simple honesty is quickly corrupted beyond recognition. When we stop telling our kids that the line between perception and truth is quintessential, we are living on the edge of lawlessness. If no one bothers to explain otherwise, life will be devalued, personal rights will take precedence over compassion, authority will be challenged, reverence will become a vestige of the past, and love will be little more than a warm, cuddly feeling.

Does any of this sound familiar?

8 David Brooks, *The Road to Character* (New York: Random House, 2015), 12.

Of course it does. These changes haven't happened overnight. As in every other era since the beginning, people of our age have found their own reasons to stop listening to God. When God is eliminated from the human dialectic, sin distorts our knowledge, our virtues, and our character. We have been living in a culture suffering from a depleted version of character for a long time.

James Davison Hunter, a distinguished professor of religion, culture, and social theory at the University of Virginia, and a popular author on the subject of Evangelicalism and cultural change in our secular age, introduced his book *The Death of Character: Moral Education without Good or Evil* with the following postmortem.

> We say we want a renewal of character in our day, but we don't really know what we ask for. To have a renewal of character is to have a renewal of a creedal order that constrains, limits, binds, obligates, and compels. This price is too high for us to pay. We want character but without unyielding conviction; we want strong morality but without the emotional burden of guilt or shame; we want virtue but without particular moral justifications that invariably offend; we want good without having to name evil; we want decency without the authority to insist upon it; we want moral community without any limitations to personal freedom. In short, we want what we cannot possibly have on the terms that we want it.[9]

A PHILOSOPHICAL CONVERSATION

A robust discussion has been gathering a head of steam in the halls of secular education. Thinkers are asking penetrating questions about our nation's moral groundings. They are reacting to the erosion of moral standards in commerce, business, medicine, politics, education, amateur and professional sports, the judicial system, and the armed forces. The evidence for this erosion is not hard to find. Moral standards (however defined) are wearing thin at work, in the marketplace, at school, online, on television, in the books we read and the films we watch. The moral erosion is real. And it is pervasive. Some argue it has already reached pandemic levels.

A new term has crept into our common vocabulary: character education (CE). The hope is that our nation's public schools will be able to right the ship of character. Stay tuned. Given the moral crises of our day, the debate is likely to attract plenty of attention over the next few decades. In a culture reticent to revisit old

9 James Davison Hunter, *The Death of Character: Moral Education in an Age without Good or Evil* (New York: Basic Books, 2000), xv.

questions about absolutes, incapable of agreeing on the seat of moral authority, and sorely lacking a reliable road map to point the way, this budding secular discussion must be understood as a nonstarter for God's people.

A HIGH-STAKES CONVERSATION

Still, the last thing many of us want is a public debate about godly character. Such a conversation is likely to raise some embarrassing questions.

The most disturbing news is the capricious way in which many of God's people circumvent this vital conversation. Just when the secular world is poised to confront some difficult moral questions, many Christian families have stopped talking at home about right and wrong, moral and immoral, good and evil. Too many parents feel inadequate, incompetent, and poorly equipped as spiritual leaders in their own homes. They are bewildered by the contradictions between their religious beliefs and the lifestyles promoted by Madison Avenue, Hollywood, Wall Street, and the popular media. Yet, they do nothing about addressing their shortcomings. Unable to make sense of these obvious contradictions, some parents have abdicated their biblical responsibility, hoping their children will encounter the faith and ethics conversation elsewhere. Others have abandoned their Bibles, deferring to popular myths and slick jargon to make sense of their troubled lives. Still others address their inner turmoil by trying to find an elusive point of balance somewhere between biblical morality and the popular, secular values that dominate the world in which they live.[10]

The stakes are high, and the cultural deck is no longer stacked in favor of the Judeo-Christian ethic. Chips on the table include friends, jobs, social opportunities, income levels, careers, and personal and professional relationships. Entire families are at risk of coming unglued by moral ambiguity. To be brutally honest, many families that once called themselves Christian are into their second or third generation of living in a godless home environment. Still, the last thing many of us want is a public debate about godly character. Such a conversation is likely to raise some embarrassing questions. At some point, we may be forced to consider the possibility that such inner conflicts may actually force the issue and give

10 Robert Kolb and Charles P. Arand, *The Genius of Luther's Theology: A Wittenberg Way of Thinking for the Contemporary Church* (Grand Rapids: Baker Academic, 2008), 13. "With Luther we must honestly confront the inevitable tendency of Christians to mix the sound of God's Word with other sounds from the world around them. Therefore, he believed that the entire life of believers, individually and as a group gathered together; the church, is a life of being called back from the way misrepresentations of reality divert us from the truth of God."

us a reason for getting serious about religion and ethics.[11] This much has to be said: whenever the conversation finally happens, it will require more courage than we've been able to muster in a half century or more.

A kind of courage that is of biblical proportion is the key for engaging in the dialogue that follows.[12] Have we forgotten to teach with words and actions Christ's moral courage in dying for us? Have we failed to notice how often Jesus tried to prepare His disciples to be courageous enough to follow His example?

This is a crucial conversation, much of which has gone missing among the people of God's church over the last few decades. If we fail to embrace it, countless steeples will be crushed by the weight of our complacency. The unadorned truth of the matter is that we are not gambling with brick and mortar investments; nor is this a noble effort to save our stately institutions or rescue the sacred principles of our republic. We are gambling with the eternal future of the blood-bought souls of our own sons and daughters. We need to be held accountable—individually and collectively—for our reckless disregard for moral rightness.

Thankfully, God forgives our lukewarm attitudes. But He is also looking for change. His desire is that we will be moved by His grace to realign our worldview with His. He promises to be with us to show us the way. That promise is accompanied by His invitation to engage Him in one of the most important conversations we will ever have.[13] May we embrace it with a humble heart.

11 Martin Galstad, *Findings: Explorations in Christian Life and Learning*, second expanded edition (Milwaukee: Wisconsin Lutheran College Press, 2008), 259. Galstad writes, "We need an education that makes people uncomfortable. They must be provoked to think. They must be stirred up."

12 For a brief Bible study on the topic of Christian courage, consider Matthew 14:27; John 19:10–11; Psalm 27:3; Isaiah 12:2; Acts 4:29.

13 See *Appendix A: Discussion Guide.*

Know therefore that the LORD *your God is God, the faithful God who keeps covenant and steadfast love with those who love Him and keep His commandments, to a thousand generations.*

—Deuteronomy 7:9

CHAPTER 2

The Blessing

Character embraces the soul,[1] but it is formed in the earthy soil of human history, human culture, and human relationships. When we stay connected to God through His Word and the Sacraments, His Spirit is also deeply involved in the shaping (and reshaping) of our worldviews. This has a spiritual effect on our day-to-day thoughts and behaviors.

But there can also be a dark side to the formation process. Character can be shaped by unbelief; that is, it can be formed in the clutches of a stifling secular culture or influenced by godless or idolatrous worldviews. In either case, while the short-term effects of its formation flow, in part, from our temporary existence on this earth, the long-term implications of having a moral character are far greater. The Bible leads us to understand this future reality after life is over in terms of heaven or hell—eternal life with God or eternal destruction in His complete absence.

1 Lyle W. Lange, *God So Loved the World* (Milwaukee: Northwestern Publishing House, 2005), 192–93. Lange writes, "The soul is immortal. . . . [The Old Testament] tells us that the functions by which life is sustained or strengthened come from the soul (Jer 31:25; Isa 55:2, 3). . . . The Bible teaches that the soul animates the body, that the soul is accountable for its actions." *Character*, on the other hand, is defined as "the attributes or features that make up and distinguish an individual." Merriam-Webster, accessed January 14, 2017, https://www.merriam-webster.com/dictionary/character.

FRAMING OUR THOUGHTS

A worldview is the distinctive, commonsense way in which we understand our world.[2] Worldviews consist of ideas and beliefs that beg interpretation, demand dialogue, and drive human interaction. They can include philosophy, assumptions, social mores, values, convictions, emotions, and ethical principles—all personal positions on a wide variety of life's most important questions. No matter how passionately entrenched these positions are, they can be vigorously argued, disagreed with, or rejected because they are not innately true or false. Worldviews are not the terminal points to life's search for meaning. They are, instead, starting points in an ongoing process that keeps us continually striving for more personal growth (however any individual might define such growth).[3] Worldviews, then, are personal understandings of how life is and how it works. Worldviews can, and frequently do, change.

Worldviews have practical applications to everyday living. In fact, they tend to govern or control just about everything we consciously say and do throughout our lives, in both a proactive sense and a reactive sense. Each individual's worldview includes a wide-ranging set of virtues, values, norms, ethical principles, and community standards that will be used as the default for making decisions about one's choices in life.[4]

Only God's people, by faith in Jesus Christ, have a worldview that can be described as godly. Jesus said, "My sheep hear My voice, and I know them, and they follow Me" (John 10:27).[5] Unbelievers don't follow Jesus. While you and I might be impressed by the good things some unbelievers do with their lives, God isn't. He is looking for perfection and holiness. Unbelievers cannot please God with their well-intended works of service and goodwill because they do not have a relationship with Jesus, the Son of God, whose perfect goodness and holiness became our goodness and holiness through faith in what He has promised to us.

---

2 Glenn S. Sunshine, *Why You Think the Way You Do: The Story of Western Worldviews from Rome to Home* (Grand Rapids: Zondervan, 2009), 14–15. Sunshine writes, "Worldview involves understanding what it means to be human . . . what you think of other people and your relationship to them. . . . Worldviews operate—below the radar, behind the scenes, guiding our thoughts, words, and actions and only rarely being examined or analyzed."

3 David J. Bosch, *Believing in the Future: Toward a Missiology of Western Culture* (Harrisburg, PA: Trinity Press International, 1995), 49.

4 In this book, "virtue" will be understood as any extension that proceeds from the Ten Commandments. "Values," on the other hand, will be understood as utilitarian and sometimes self-serving extensions of human wisdom. Even by this definition, Scripture holds some values in high esteem. See *Appendix B: Biblical Character.*

5 For a brief Bible study on the topic of faith, see Hebrews 11:1, 6; Romans 1:17; 5:1; Galatians 3:6; Philippians 4:7–9; John 6:28–29; 20:27; Proverbs 3:5; 29:25.

One of the Bible's most compelling examples of godly character formation is found in the case of a man named Moses. Our quest for understanding the essence of biblical character and its formation begins with an event from Moses' life.

WHAT'S IN A NAME?

Sheep have a one-track mind. A sheep's sole purpose in life is to satisfy the unrelenting hunger gnawing in its belly. As a shepherd, Moses would have understood his flock's passion for grazing. He also would have known how his sheep were incapable of making plans to abandon an overgrazed hillside to go in search of greener pastures. Instead, when their food source dwindled, they would one-by-one foolishly wander off with no concern for their own safety. Those that did not perish from hunger would soon become protein on some wild beast's menu.

A good shepherd is constantly in search of fresh vegetation for his flock. While sheep relate to their shepherd, their yearning for meaningful relationships with other sheep is rather limited. Sheep have no permanent home. With the possible exception of their early drive to seek their mother's milk, family means almost nothing to a sheep, nor does the loyalty of friendship. But the many weeks of solitude with his flock likely would have left Moses longing for companionship with other people. Unlike sheep, a man must belong. People are drawn to other people. We exchange ideas, foster each other's dreams, reflect, plan, share, and learn from one another. We need one another to be reassured that our life matters to somebody. We need other people in our lives to certify us as card-carrying members of the human race.

Like all humans, Moses would have relied on others to give meaning and purpose to his life. In his youth, Moses had the rare experience of assimilating two very different cultures. As an infant, he had been exposed to the culture of his Hebrew family. At the feet of his Hebrew mother, young Moses learned to trust in the God of his forefathers—Abraham, Isaac, and Jacob. He worshiped the one true God.

But Moses was also raised with a royal pedigree. Pharaoh's daughter had adopted him as an infant, saving him from certain death. As an adopted member of Pharaoh's household, Moses became acquainted with privilege and power. In Pharaoh's house, he learned about new technologies. He was taught to cipher word symbols, a gift that would become necessary later in life, when Moses would author the inspired first five books of the Bible.

In Pharaoh's court, religious cults touted the Nile Valley's most powerful deities—Osiris, Ra, Horus, Isis. Moses was likely familiar with them all. He knew, too, that each ruling dynasty favored a different god or goddess, and that all of Egypt's gods and goddesses served at the will of the ruling pharaoh. Perhaps he wondered how it was possible for a deity to be subject to the whims of a human king. God was clearly never ruled by the whims of His own human creatures.

The two cultures that defined Moses were polar opposites. They gave him a rich understanding of two very different ways of life. But his mixed cultural background likely often clashed deep within, as though the gods of Egypt were at war with the true God. Whatever his spiritual and cultural tensions were, Moses finally exploded in moral outrage over an Egyptian taskmaster's inhumane treatment of a Hebrew slave. He knew immorality when he saw it, murdering the brute in cold blood, burying the body in a shallow grave. When his felony was exposed, Moses fled into the desert, where, working for his father-in-law as a shepherd, he would spend the next forty years wandering from one watering hole to another. One can imagine that during the long, lonely nights, Moses must have contemplated his rash act of taking another man's life.

One day, Moses decided to turn his father-in-law's flock toward a mountain range called Sinai. There, on the slopes of a peak named Horeb, the mountain of God, a bush flared into a fireball. This happened every now and then in the dry desert heat. Only this bush was not consumed. Curious, Moses began to approach the bush. Scripture continues this way,

> When the Lord saw that he turned aside to see, God called to him out of the bush, "Moses, Moses!"
>
> And he said, "Here I am."
>
> Then He said, "Do not come near; take your sandals off your feet, for the place on which you are standing is holy ground." And He said, "I am the God of your father, the God of Abraham, the God of Isaac, and the God of Jacob." And Moses hid his face, for he was afraid to look at God. Then the Lord said, "I have surely seen the affliction of My people who are in Egypt and have heard their cry because of their taskmasters. I know their sufferings, and I have come down to deliver them out of the hand of the Egyptians and to bring them up out of that land to a good and broad land, a land flowing with milk and honey. . . ."
>
> God said to Moses, "I am who I am." And He said, "Say this to the people of Israel: 'I am has sent me to you.'" God also said to Moses, "Say this to the people of Israel: 'The Lord, the God of your fathers, the God of Abraham, the God of Isaac, and the God of Jacob, has

> sent me to you.' This is My name forever, and thus I am to be remembered throughout all generations."[6] (Exodus 3:4–8, 14–15)

Later, Moses pleaded that he would need a sign to convince the people. I AM[7] gave Moses several miracles that would serve as his calling card. When Moses tried to make the case that he had a thick tongue and didn't think well on his feet, I AM said He would teach Moses what to say and how to speak with authority. When Moses begged God to give the job to someone else, I AM said He would arrange to have Moses' brother Aaron be his spokesman. Moses' petty excuses were infuriating. Yet, the Lord met each of Moses' challenges with holy patience. When the conversation ended, Moses tried to make sense of what had just happened. He knew his life had changed. Soon he would be shepherding God's chosen people on a forty-year pilgrimage through the Sinai wilderness.

If you and I are ever to know who we are, we will need to hear a voice in the wilderness. To understand human character, one must begin where I AM began, with something as basic as a name.

Becoming a parent is a life-changing experience. Much thought goes into the naming of a new family member. Names are the hooks on which people hang the details of character. We remember one another by name, address others by name, relate to one another by name. Our good names vouch for our integrity. Names matter.

Scripture teaches us about our God through the many divine names that reveal His being. The I AM name for God, for example, reveals some of the Divinity's most important characteristics. It identifies our loving God as the eternal One, whose limitless mercy and boundless grace is complete in every way and free of any quid pro quo demands.

At the beginning of our lives, you and I had to rely on others to choose a name for us. Most of us were named by our parents. God has no parents. He has no beginning. I AM is timeless, eternal. Furthermore, God needs no one to tell Him who He is or to share ideas about virtue or character with Him. He is His own Counselor, independent in every sense. Sovereign. Not bound by any laws or boundaries. He knows His purpose and how to achieve His mission. He makes His own decisions, and they are all perfectly consistent with His loving identity.[8]

---

6 God insists we keep His name sacred, using it with reverence and living in a way that brings honor, praise, and glory to it. See Exodus 20:7.

7 The *Concordia Self-Study Bible* (St. Louis: Concordia Publishing House, 1986), 90. In Hebrew, this name for God is written with four letters—*YHWH*. Common English renderings are *Jehovah* or *Yahweh*. This is "The name by which God wished to be known and worshiped in Israel—the name that expresses his character as the dependable and faithful God who desires the full trust of his people."

8 God's essential identity is love. See 1 John 4:16.

Our God will never forget, modify, alter, or undo the promises He has made to us. Never.

He is perfectly good. He always exists in the present. In Revelation, John hears Christ Jesus, the Son of God, identify Himself: "I am the Alpha and the Omega . . . who *is* and who *was* and who *is to come*, the Almighty" (Revelation 1:8, emphasis added). This is a beautiful reminder that God is not captive to time. He transcends it. In our past, God always *is*. In our future, He always *is*. In our ephemeral present, He is.

If you think about this too long, it will probably give you a headache. The concept is nearly incomprehensible for human beings who have never spent a single nanosecond outside the dimensions of time and space. Before we've had a chance to enjoy it, the present we have waited for so patiently has already become history, and a winsome soul observes how "time flies."

The ongoing passage of time also keeps changing our perspective. A fifty-year-old doesn't think or act like an eighteen-year-old. An eighteen-year-old doesn't reason or behave like a two-year-old. We are constantly generating new ideas, gaining new understandings, experiencing new sensations. Who can claim to be the same person today that he or she was last year, yesterday, or even a minute ago?

God's perspective never changes. His will is not influenced by the rising or falling of the tides, the changing seasons, shifts in world power, or the turn of a screw. In a world gone berserk with change, this is very comforting news. Our God will never forget, modify, alter, or undo the promises He has made to us.[9] Never.

It takes some effort to tease all this from God's Yahweh name. The prophet Malachi quoted God simply and directly: "I the Lord do not change" (Malachi 3:6). The author of the general letter to the Hebrew Christians connects this same quality to the God-man, Jesus, writing, "Jesus Christ is the same yesterday and today and forever" (Hebrews 13:8). And, speaking of Himself, Jesus declared, "Truly, truly, I say to you, before Abraham was, I am" (John 8:58).

Change is a constant of God's created universe. When He called light out of the everlasting darkness, the documenting of change began. We call it history (some people like to think of it as His Story). In the beginning, our timeless, spaceless, and changeless Creator fashioned His human creatures to fit perfectly into an environment of ongoing change. And lest we forget, change has been an integral part of His plan to intervene in mankind's sinful condition. Without the divine invention, which effects a spiritual change, we are all doomed.

9 The technical term used to describe God's unchanging character is "immutable."

Change is a constant of our lives. We cannot escape its reality. It is also a necessary component of character formation.[10] Our conversation will include lots of discussions about change.

THE ORIGIN OF CHARACTER

Inspired by God's almighty power, Moses wrote the narrative that explains how the cosmic universe came to be.[11] On the very first page of Genesis, he tells us that God spoke.[12] When God spoke, things like gravity, stars, fish, insects, birds, supernovas, trees, the laws of nature, bodies of water, hippopotamuses, and flowers appeared. It would seem, from what we can tell from Moses' narrative, that many aspects of the created cosmos were finished, in full form, functional in every detail, and thoroughly equipped for living in the new time, space, and change environment that God was here creating.

Creating something from nothing with a few spoken words seems perfectly natural for a God as mighty and powerful as ours, until one realizes that no one was around at the moment of creation to actually hear what God was saying. This raises an interesting question: Why would God want us to know that His creative work came about with the utterance of a few human words? Perhaps this was His way of reminding human beings that He holds the patent to the universe's cosmic design. Or He may be telling us that He made the props, built the set, outlined the plot, designed the lighting, wrote the script, determined the subplots, fleshed out the characters, and decided how, when, and where each actor would appear on stage. Is He reminding us that He is Master Architect of all things and we are not?[13] And, while we mull over these questions, consider what a wonder it is that He wrote us (you, me, the entire human race) into His eternal script. By communicating in a human language, God was actually making His story our story and telling His human creatures that His story and our stories are forever inseparable.

10 Alison Gopnik, *The Philosophical Baby: What Children's Minds Tell Us about Truth, Love, and the Meaning of Life* (London: The Bodley Head; Random House, 2009), 6–8. Gopnik writes, "More than any other creature, human beings are able to change. . . . Our capacity for instigating change, both in our own lives and through history, is the most distinctive and unchanging thing about us. . . . We change our surroundings and our surroundings change us. We alter other people's behavior, their behavior alters us. We begin with the capacity to learn more effectively and more flexibly about our environment than any other species. This knowledge lets us imagine new environments, and act to change the existing ones." Alison Gopnik is a contemporary British child-development researcher and a popular author/lecturer.

11 God inspired Moses to write the first five books of the Bible.

12 *Genesis* means "beginning."

13 Isaiah used the inspired metaphor of the potter and his clay to express the simple truth that God is God and we are not. See Isaiah 29:16; 45:9; 64:8.

God is a relational being. He loves to communicate. In Genesis 1:26, we read about a high-level convocation involving the three persons of the Trinity. There is not a hint of disagreement, jealousy, rancor, or ill will—only perfect unity. The Father is speaking. "Let Us make man in Our image, after Our likeness." Our triune God is contemplating the next creative act.[14] (Remember, God serves as His own wise counsel.)

Being a relational creature is also fundamental to the formation of human character. In this respect, humans are very much like their Creator. Our relationships with one another are a necessary aspect of God's plan to have His human creatures serve as blessings for one another.[15] In God's world, we are never alone.[16] Our discussion will spend plenty of energy considering our relationships and their important role in making us the people we are as God's people.

A FORMULA FOR CHARACTER

Genesis 1:26 continues with the divine decision to "let them have dominion over the fish of the sea and over the birds of the heavens and over the livestock and over all the earth and over every creeping thing that creeps on the earth." The words "have dominion" are particularly significant. They make us think of similar terms such as "rule," "care for," "govern," "watch over." God wanted His human creatures to manage His creation—an honor and a privilege that Adam had done nothing to earn or deserve.

This caretaker's role had the effect of adding another dimension to the complex character of humankind. God wanted His human creatures to be people of action—to make decisions, have responsibility, plan, execute our plans, work, play, and rest. He wanted people to have purposeful lives that would give them opportunities to express their love for Him and for one another.[17] Human character

---

14 Carl J. Lawrenz and John C. Jeske, *A Commentary on Genesis 1–11* (Milwaukee: Northwestern Publishing House, 2004), 75. Lawrenz and Jeske write, "Bearing God's image indeed presupposes a personality possessing self-consciousness and a fully developed intellect. But these features in themselves are not yet the divine image. According to Scripture, human beings have lost the image of God through the fall into sin, even though they still remain rational, self-conscious personalities."

15 Kolb and Arand, *Genius*, 26–27. These authors write, "Integral to his design, God created us as relational beings (in Luther's academic Latin, *in relatione*) who live in his presence (*coram Deo*) and at the same time in community with one another (*coram mundo*)."

16 Hauerwas, *Peaceable Kingdom*, 97. Hauerwas writes, "Our individuality is possible only because we are first of all social beings. After all, the 'self' names not a thing, but a relation. I know who I am only in relation to others, and, indeed, who I am is a relation with others."

17 Lawrenz and Jeske, *Genesis 1–11*, 73–74. Lawrenz and Jeske write, "All of the earth's powers and resources—physical, chemical, electrical, and atomic—were placed under their jurisdiction. This dominion has not been withdrawn from man. It has, however, been greatly modified by man's fall into sin. Sinful depravity now causes mankind to abuse and misuse and exploit this God-given dominion. . . . As long as man bore the image of God, there was no danger that he would misuse or abuse God's creation."

would be a combination of being and doing.[18] The Creator's design for human character can now be expressed as a formula that defines us in a way that will be helpful later. The formula is **C = I + P**: Character equals Identity plus Performance.[19]

The formula is C = I + P: Character equals Identity plus Performance.

In giving humankind this purposeful task, the Lord was also giving the gift of worth to His human creatures. And, as if this were not enough, God also gave the human race the intellect, talent, skills, and vision to carry out the administrative tasks that God would assign.

Then we are told, "God blessed them" (Genesis 1:28). This happens so fast, and sounds so right, that the moment can easily be missed. And it often is. In these three little words, God is already reaching out to mankind with selfless love, setting the tone for every word of the Bible's sixty-six books. From that moment on, the fountain of His blessings has never stopped flowing. Yet, with but a single exception, humankind has never done a single thing to deserve or earn His blessings. Moreover, this first mention of the blessings God pours out to His special human creatures is directly tied to our ability to multiply. God wants many generations to know who He is (His identity) and what He has done (His performance).

God loves people—all of them—including those who have not yet been conceived. If He were to walk away from His favorite creatures, He would be in conflict with His own loving nature. He wants to know all people intimately and personally. And He wants them to know Him in the same loving way.[20] If you and I really want to understand ourselves better, we will first need to get to know our Creator's love for us.

---

18 This book uses the word "identity" to refer to our existential "being": name, origin, and any substantive elements of a human being (physical, emotional, intellectual, etc). It uses the term "performance" in reference to our abilities and capacities relating to behaviors of "doing."

19 The respected contemporary Lutheran theologian Robert Kolb used "identity" and "performance" to express his understanding of passive and active righteousness. We first saw the formula C = I + P being used to depict human character in a devotion presented by Matthew Hoehner.

20 Kolb and Arand, *Genius*, 222–223. Kolb and Arand write, "Luther's faith viewed reality in an intensely personal way. For him, God is a person who wants to be conversing with his human creatures, who live in communion or community with both God and other creatures, human and nonhuman. Luther also held to a radical distinction between the Creator and his creatures. This led him to presume, quite naturally, that God had designed him and all other human beings to be in a relationship of dependence and trust with the one who had crafted them."

But to all who did receive Him, who believed in His name, He gave the right to become children of God, who were born, not of blood nor of the will of the flesh nor of the will of man, but of God.

—John 1:12–13

CHAPTER 3

How Character Is Formed

There are no shortcuts; forming character takes time. Though the first few years of a child's life are the most critical, character formation actually takes a lifetime.[1]

While no two parents approach child-rearing in exactly the same way, the pattern for character formation is remarkably consistent from child to child and in family after family. While many of us are ill prepared for the parental role, character of some kind still emerges.[2] This is because the structure and instinctive drive that make the process percolate are already in place at birth. *Family*—which today is often defined in a number of ways—provides the structure.[3] In a pluralistic society, our contemporary culture has struggled to arrive at a consensus for the definition of family. *Learning*—which under the auspices of formal education has undergone remarkable changes in the last two hundred years—drives the process forward.

---

1 Gopnik, *Philosophical Baby*, 5. Gopnik writes, "Babies can't walk or talk, and even toddlers, well, toddle, and yet science, and indeed common sense, tell us that in those early years they are learning more than they ever will again. . . . In some ways, young children are actually smarter, more imaginative, more caring, and even more conscious than adults are."

2 George Barna, *Revolutionary Parenting: Raising Your Kids to Become Spiritual Champions* (Carol Stream, IL: Tyndale House, 2007), xvii. Barna writes, "Most parents are not prepared to be effective in their roles. They often lack the self-confidence needed to fully invest themselves in the process. Consequently, they seek individuals and organizations to help them handle the burden of shaping their child's life in positive ways."

3 For a brief Bible study about family, see Genesis 1:28; 2:24; Psalm 68:5–6a; 127:3; Mark 3:34–35; Ephesians 6:1–4; 2 Corinthians 6:18; and 1 John 3:1. For a brief Bible study about learning, see Luke 2:52; 1 Corinthians 13:11; Deuteronomy 6:1–9; and Proverbs 22:6.

In Scripture, both family and learning are presented as extraordinary blessings. They may seem rather ordinary to us because their wonder often gets lost in the incremental, plodding progress that children make on their way to becoming adults. We take the great mystery of character formation so much for granted that we rarely bother to think about how our moral compasses are constructed. In this chapter, we will examine the formation process in four separate phases that, in real life, are more often quite difficult to distinguish.

THE BLESSING OF NEW LIFE

Character formation begins with a mother and her newborn baby. Rooted in biology, an emotional attachment soon follows as the mother cuddles, nurtures, and protects her infant. This bond is the infant's first cultural experience.[4]

Soon after birth, the child's community expands to include other people: care-giving nurses, the child's father, siblings, grandparents, aunts, uncles, cousins, and friends of the family. Many of these individuals will have a hand in shaping the infant's early character. But, by virtue of their roles in bringing this new life into the world, the child's mother and father share the primary responsibility for contributing to their offspring's early understanding of life.[5]

Good parents love their children. Godly parents show how much they love their children by starting them out on their lifelong path to heaven by leading them to their Savior. This is in keeping with God's plan. He has positioned parents as His personal envoys for raising God-fearing children. To meet this challenge, He gives parents a measure of authority to help them carry out their leadership role. Along with the honor connected to the position, a parent also assumes profound responsibilities. As the decision makers in their infant's early life, parents can expect to make many conscious choices on their child's behalf. Later, as the child grows to adulthood, the decision-making responsibility will be transferred to the young, maturing adult.

One of the first decisions Christian parents should make on behalf of their child is to introduce the spiritual influence of God's Holy Spirit in their baby's young life. God wants to have a rich, personal relationship with every child. It is in every child's best spiritual interest to receive God's gift of faith as early as possible through the miracle of Baptism.

---

4 We tend to think that cultures consist of artifacts generated by large populations over long periods of time. A culture can be that. A culture can also be the interaction of as few as two people, such as a mother and her child, or a handful of believers who worship God together.

5 We will not want to leave the door open for any misinterpretation that suggests the primary burden for the spiritual training of children lies with either the church or the state. Both the church and the state have a stake in child-rearing, but God has given the primary onus of this responsibility to parents. (See Deuteronomy 6 and 11.)

In Baptism, God gives new life to a sinner who deserves only God's angry punishment for sin. In God's holy name and with the application of ordinary water, a baptized child receives God's full and complete forgiveness and the promise of everlasting life in heaven. In Baptism, He promises a lifetime of peace through the reassuring knowledge that He has claimed this child as a member of His own dear family of believers. That promise comes from Jesus' own lips: "Whoever believes and is baptized will be saved, but whoever does not believe will be condemned" (Mark 16:16).[6]

God wants parents to train their children to live in obedience to His commandments and to know that He alone is the God of their salvation.

God also provides an impressive array of resources to support parents in their difficult task. This warehouse of divine assets includes prayer, the child's conscience, the Ten Commandments and the rest of Luther's Small Catechism, the support and encouragement of other members of God's family of believers, and all of God's inspired Word.[7]

Parental participation in a child's spiritual growth is not optional.[8] God's first blessing of His human creatures (Genesis 1:28) was carefully wrapped in the concept that each generation bears the responsibility for passing God's love on to next generation.

After the fall, the Creator promised to send a Savior for all the generations. Ever since, He has been telling moms and dads to teach His promises to their children and not to forget what He has done for them. God wants parents to train their children to live in obedience to His commandments and to know that He alone is the God of their salvation. In household after household, His desire is for parents to surround their children with His unconditional love.

While the Bible does not counsel parents for every possible circumstance, it does provide clear statements that set moral boundaries. These statements are

---

6 Kenneth R. Kratz, *The Word Speaks: 365 Devotions Based on the Sayings of Jesus* (Milwaukee: Northwestern Publishing House, 2011), 15. Kratz writes, "Each child born from two human parents has a sinful nature. Jesus said, 'Flesh gives birth to flesh, but the Spirit gives birth to spirit' (John 3:6). Sinful human beings give birth to sinful human beings. Each baby born is desperately corrupt before God and without any spiritual life. That is why we need to be born again. Neither an infant nor an adult can produce spiritual life within the heart. . . . Only the almighty power of the Spirit can bring life to a spiritually dead heart."

7 Kolb and Arand, *Genius*, 23. "We learn our presuppositions about who we are at our core from our parents and the surrounding world, which has been shaped by the prevailing currents in church, university, and society."

8 Spiritual training should emphasize the application of God's truth to everyday life. The daily life of a Christian household includes spiritual activities such as daily repentance, worship, family prayer, reading and discussing God's Word together, forgiving one another, and observing religious festivals.

intended to be used to direct the application of Bible truth to the daily lives of His people. The gathering phase is prime time for Christian parents to teach basic Bible truths.

THE GATHERING PHASE

One of the best ways to teach godly virtues to young children is to focus on the Bible's many narratives. Regardless of the amount of biblical training that Christian parents have had as children, it is worth the time and energy to relearn these narratives as adults. God intended these stories for adults as much as He intended them for children. Moreover, godly parents can't help their children grow spiritually if they are not also growing. New insights, drawn from an adult perspective, can make these Bible lessons more meaningful for parents and children alike. It also helps parents become more aware of the rich themes of Scripture, where word pictures begin to connect together the truths in God's Word.

Regardless of the amount of biblical training that Christian parents have had as children, it is worth the time and energy to relearn these narratives as adults.

A child's cognitive awareness is like a sponge. In this stage, kids are ready to be saturated with many moral ideas.[9] But the gathering process is generally quite random. Ethical material is normally collected in a helter-skelter fashion, without the benefit of filters or a safety net. It is an exciting time, filled with discovery, optimism, and fanciful thoughts. But young children are naively inclined to trust almost anyone. Some human ideas about right and wrong are insidiously godless. Conscientious Christian parents are right to be cautious about the moral ideas to which their children are being exposed. The standard Christian parents need to use for establishing clear moral lines for their children is not negotiable. That foundational standard is God's Ten Commandments. Throughout Scripture, the Ten Commandments are supported as the clearest and most concise expression of God's holy will.

Adolescents need to hear that life is filled with choices, and that the choices they make in life will bring either shame or glory to God's name. God's Ten Commandments are a clear expression of His will for the way we conduct our lives. The secular version of moral living is more interested in preserving a way of life on earth that is filled with opportunities for self-advancement. Christian parents will not only want to teach the substance of the Ten Commandments, but they will also want to teach their children to wisely apply each commandment to godly

9 Learning of this kind is often described as being "more caught than taught."

living, both in the negative sense of "thou shalt not" and in the positive sense of "lov[ing] your neighbor as yourself" (Matthew 22:39).

Commandments 1 through 3 speak about our relationship with God. This aspect of human relationships is ignored in secular worldviews. Commandments 4 through 10 focus on our human relationships. God's Fourth Commandment, for example, includes a discussion about authority and our relationships with those who govern the various communities on earth. Godly parents train their children to respect their nation's laws and honor the authority of people whom God has placed into a leadership position over a nation, a family, a business, a civic organization, a military unit, a church, a school, or a classroom.

Some of the Bible's most basic principles are so important they warrant being taught and retaught. One of these principles is the simple truth that Jesus is with us at all times and wherever we go. Children sometimes find this truth hard to believe because they cannot see Jesus. As their tiny faith grows, they begin to realize that they actually can see Jesus in their hearts and through the spiritual eyes of faith.

A second Bible truth that all children should hear daily is that God loves them and, for Jesus' sake, forgives them when they have done something wrong. This is also a good time for parents to remind their children of their mother's and father's love for them. This includes a reminder that a godly parent's love is unconditional, and so is their forgiveness for any and all wrongdoing.

All children should learn the Bible narrative that explains what Jesus did for them on Calvary's cross. This narrative is emphasized during every Church Year's season of Lent and Holy Week. The Church Year cycle gives parents many opportunities to tell and retell familiar Bible narratives. It is a good practice to spend time discussing these important narratives with children, not only to review the facts but also to understand the depth of God's love for sinners. With each annual repetition of the same wonderful stories, parents can explore a new facet of the simple truths embedded in each narrative.

Forming character in children combines parental instruction and modeling. When parents lead a moral life, God gives them many opportunities to be godly examples for their children. But the models we provide will never be perfect, because all parents are sinners. Our children need to be able to see us finding peace from our guilt and receiving God's assurance that we are forgiven. We confess our sins publicly in a general confession during corporate worship. When appropriate, we should also seek God's help and be encouraged to admit our guilt to our children when we have said or done something wrong.

The Bible frequently stretches our thoughts beyond our finite reality on earth by confronting us with concepts that transcend the natural world of time, space, and change. Jesus called this spiritual reality "the kingdom of God" or "the kingdom of heaven."[10]

God's kingdom introduces us to the spiritual reality of angels and demons, miracles, the devil, prayer, heaven, and hell. In God's kingdom, we learn to appreciate the incredibly wonderful news that we will live forever in the new heavens and the new earth. His kingdom is a spiritual reality that Jesus says exists within us.[11] He invites us to find lasting peace, forgiveness, comfort, hope, courage, guidance, love, acceptance, joy, purpose, and meaning—to find God and to learn to trust His sure promises.

God's kingdom is discernible to a child who has the spiritual eyes and ears of faith through the power of Baptism. Faith grasps God's reality tightly and holds on for dear life. Faith, not reason, is where Christian parents will want to take their first stand.[12]

Moses told Hebrew parents how God wanted them to train their children. Contemporary Christian parents are blessed to be able to apply this same principle to our own families in the twenty-first century.

> These words that I command you today shall be on your heart. You shall teach them diligently to your children, and shall talk of them when you sit in your house, and when you walk by the way, and when you lie down, and when you rise. You shall bind them as a sign on your hand, and they shall be as frontlets between your eyes. You shall write them on the doorposts of your house and on your gates. (Deuteronomy 6:6–9)

THE TESTING PHASE

Children typically shift their attention from harvesting to testing between ages 8 and 10. (Girls often begin this phase a few years before boys.) The intellectual

---

10 Matthew alternately uses the expressions "the kingdom of God" and "the kingdom of heaven" to talk about the same concept. However, the latter expression leads to some confusion because of our contemporary understanding of the word *heaven*. Today, *heaven* implies the eternal hereafter. In the context of God's kingdom, that definition leads to the common misunderstanding that God's kingdom exists exclusively in the future tense of eternity, that is, after Judgment Day. The Bible teaches that God's people are already experiencing a foretaste of His kingdom in their heart of faith, even while they are still living on earth.

11 See Luke 17:20–21.

12 Siegbert W. Becker, *The Foolishness of God: The Place of Reason in the Theology of Martin Luther* (Milwaukee: Northwestern Publishing House, 1982), 7. Becker quotes Martin Luther: "Reason is incapable of discovering and incompetent to judge religious truth. Reason has its place in the area of natural science, and it can render a service even in theology, but it has absolutely no business 'to investigate the origin of the whole world, where it came from and where it is going, whether it has a beginning or existed from eternity, whether there is a supreme being over the world, who rules all things.'"

capacity of young adolescents, coupled with their increased life experience, prepares them for considering serious questions. The time has come for separating the ethical wheat from chaff.

To get a better sense of how this winnowing process works, imagine a trip to the local grocery. Being a fruit lover, you head for the fresh fruit section and begin placing apples, oranges, grapefruit, pears, mangoes, cantaloupes, pineapples, bananas, plums, grapes, and strawberries into your shopping cart. Then, you realize you forgot to check for freshness, soft spots, signs of rot or mildew. If you don't take the time now to examine each fruit, you'll be disappointed when you get home. So, you unpack the cart. Some fruits have to be discarded because they don't smell fresh. Others are bruised. You notice the mangoes are overpriced and return them to the shelf. But some fruits pass the test. You head for the checkout line, confident about the choices you've made.

Of course, we are not talking about purchasing fruit. We are talking about children embracing the moral material that will be used in constructing their character. When this phase is completed, the bits and pieces of the moral convictions still standing will be the bones for a teen's understanding of right and wrong. As an adult, this frame will serve as a mature worldview. Minor adjustments may still be made. But it will require something like an earthquake measuring 8.2 on the Richter scale to cause significant change in the worldviews of young people who have completed this stage.

In the testing phase, adolescents either validate or discard the moral concepts they harvested as a child. A red flag is raised when an adolescent observes immoral behavior in the same person who first introduced him or her to a conflicting virtue as a child.

Parents often carry a heavy burden during their adolescent's testing phase. Moms and dads, who have contributed the lion's share of the moral material their child once harvested, are now the object of the same child's relentless testing. Just when most parents are beginning to think they have lost most of their influence in their child's life, their adolescent is busily trying to decide which of the ethical concepts his or her parents have passed down are valuable enough to use in the building of a fully functional moral compass.

For this phase of the formation process, moms and dads generally need to be rowing in the same direction. Some kids can rise above a situation in which their parents are sending mixed messages of clashing ethical principles. Many cannot. When a child senses that his loyalties are being divided between a moral principle he took from one parent, only to be contradicted by the other parent's rejection of that same moral truth, he will feel he is being forced to choose between his father and mother. Many young people are crushed under such pressure.

It takes work for parents to get on the same moral page.

It takes work for parents to get on the same moral page. Thankfully, God's Commandments establish a sound moral foundation for godly moms, dads, and their children.

This is a good time to make the point that, while parenting is a lifelong task, a time will come when parents need to back away from active participation in the formation process. David L. Reuter writes:

> In Philippians 1:6, Paul reminds us that God will bring our faith to completion. Our work teaching our children is something we will never complete, and that is just as God has planned. It is not our job to bring their training to completion. We will be the primary shapers of their faith from a human standpoint. However, God began and will complete the good work of faith in our lives and in the lives of our children. Therefore, each time we prepare to teach a faith lesson to our children, we should pray that our words might be God's Word, and that we might faithfully assist in the formation of faith that God is accomplishing in our children's lives.[13]

THE ORDERING PHASE

Our Creator is a God of order. None of us should be surprised to learn that He hardwired His human creatures with an appreciation for order. During the ordering phase, validated virtues will be fixed in a hierarchy of moral convictions. Some individuals will take longer to complete the validating process, making it difficult to predict when this third phase will typically shift into high gear.

Ranked virtues help young adults make tough moral decisions. But the ranking system does not do its work alone. It works in tandem with the child's conscience.[14]

Everyone has a conscience, believers and unbelievers alike. The consciences of some individuals can be more active than the consciences of others. Some people try to switch their consciences off to avoid feeling guilt. When people try to silence their conscience, it is as though they have removed the batteries from a warning device that God gave them to tell them that something is morally wrong with their decision making.

---

13 David L. Reuter, *Teaching the Faith at Home: What Does This Mean? How Is This Done?* (St. Louis: Concordia Publishing House, 2016), 217.

14 We do not mean to imply that one's conscience first begins to develop during this phase. Young children can have a very active conscience, even as they are gathering and testing new moral concepts.

Our conscience is a kind of self-talk—an internal conversation, triggered when a moral decision is under consideration. Theologians sometimes describe our conscience as the shadowy remains of the clear and perfect understanding of God's will. Cartoonists have pictured an active conscience as an angelic figure sitting on one shoulder, making a (biblical) case for choosing the right path in a moral issue. A devilish figure sits on the other shoulder, tempting the person to take the path marked "wicked." Making light of the devil, or flirting with the lies he tells, is like whistling in a cemetery in the dark. The father of lies is a formidable enemy. He has the power to undermine people's faith in God's promises. That said, the cartoon depiction is a fairly good representation of the battle that is going on within the individual who is struggling with a moral choice. A more refined way of describing it is as a battle between our old, sinful flesh (called our old Adam) and the transformed believer's desire to live according to God's will (referred to as our new man in Christ). The new man dominates the internal conversation, but sometimes the old Adam convinces us that the evil we are contemplating isn't as immoral or as deadly as we think. If the choice is to follow the counsel of our old Adam, the conscience accuses and convicts the sinner, urging the individual to repent.

So far, we have emphasized the important role that others play in the gathering and testing phases of character formation. When it comes to the influence of one's conscience, the role others have played in acquiring a godly character becomes background.[15] For an active conscience, the choice to do good or evil becomes a very personal matter.

We are all born with a conscience.[16] An infant's conscience is largely inactive because a baby's brain is incapable of making rational choices. But the child's spiritual bent is already hostile to God. Even then, an infant's natural, sinful worldview has already done the mean work of blunting the effectiveness of this remarkable spiritual tool.[17] In effect, we all begin life with our moral arms tied behind our backs.

---

15 Richard Sorabji, *Moral Conscience through the Ages: Fifth Century BCE to the Present* (Chicago: University of Chicago Press, 2014), 11–12. According to Sorabji, "The Greek expression which came to be the standard term for conscience began to appear with some of its eventual meaning in the playwrights of the fifth century BCE. It involved a metaphor of one sharing knowledge with oneself, as if one were split into two. The shared knowledge is of a defect, and usually, except in Plato, of a moral defect. . . . The standard meaning involves one's own knowledge of one's own fault." [Sorabji credits the latter portion of his statement to C. A. Pierce, *Conscience in the New Testament*, ch. 3, p. 38.]

16 Lange, *God So Loved*, 102–3. Lange writes, "When Adam and Eve fell into sin, the knowledge of the law was clouded but not obliterated. The conscience, a spiritual emotion within us, testifies that we are accountable to God for our actions. It either approves of what we do or condemns us for what we do (Ro 2:14–15)."

17 The theological term for the lethal spiritual condition all human beings inherit at conception is original sin.

Sharpening a child's conscience and helping a child reach moral maturity is an important part of a Christian parent's training regimen. The argument that it is cruel to burden a child's conscience is not supported by Scripture. Loving correction is a critical aspect of God's mandate to parents. On the other hand, correcting children with cruel words or harsh punishments is never acceptable, either to God or to society.

God wants Christian parents to plant His Law deep in the hearts of their children. He wants our children to develop a conscience with the moral torque to hold them accountable to His Law. He wants to be understood as our Judge, to be known as the loving and forgiving heavenly Father, and He wants us to turn to Him for the moral strength to overcome temptation.

THE SHARING PHASE

Sharing is quintessential to the human experience. Someone once said, "We grow by giving ourselves away." What wise words those are! The parental task becomes exponentially more exciting when children at an early age learn to share themselves with others.

Age actually has less to do with selfless sharing than one might think. Young children are just as capable of giving themselves away as adults. It happens quite naturally when children see their parents being generous and making sacrifices on behalf of others.

Godly parents share themselves when they live as the salt of the earth and light of the world (Matthew 5:13–16). Helping a child's faith grow to maturity is the most valuable extension of self that any parent can offer. Carrying out our role as Christian parents places us on a growth curve of our own. Children need to see us sitting at Jesus' feet, going to church regularly, attending Bible class, and reading our Bibles at home.

CHARACTER AND CULTURE

Though the plan for character formation, along with the tools to make it happen, come from God, the process doesn't always go smoothly. Sometimes it isn't even linear. Character usually forms in a herky-jerky rhythm, with awkward starts and unexpected fits of regression. It can be clumsy, uncomfortable, challenging, frustrating, disappointing, depressing, costly, and messy. This is because human relationships can be messy. Nonetheless, character never forms in a vacuum. Our relation-

Our relationships, rooted in our relationship with our loving Lord Jesus, are the critical mass that God uses to get the job of character formation done.

ships, rooted in our relationship with our loving Lord Jesus, are the critical mass that God uses to get the job of character formation done. Our homes are His preferred culture for getting a good head start.

For the time is coming when people will not endure sound teaching, but having itching ears they will accumulate for themselves teachers to suit their own passions.

—2 Timothy 4:3

CHAPTER 4

A Siren's Song

To the test question "What is culture?" one student wrote, "Culture is the spark ignited when two or more people rub their ideas together." While the answer sounds a bit glib, it was actually not a bad response. The definition of human culture must certainly acknowledge the human capacity to use existing understandings to formulate new ideas.

There's always another new idea coming around the bend that could make our kids rethink their values, question their purpose, doubt their identity, or undermine their convictions.

Americans tend to be optimistic about new ideas. Invention, ingenuity, and imagination are our most important measures of contemporary progress. New ideas fuel our hope for a better tomorrow. Some people believe the real currency of the future is neither money nor time, but is rather the currency of an active imagination. That said, not all new ideas are good ideas. In spite of our national fervor for being on the cutting edge, discerning parents should occasionally wince when they hear about some of the latest trends. There's always another new idea coming around the bend that could make our kids rethink their values, question their purpose, doubt their identity, or undermine their convictions. Our conversation turns to exploring *why* and *how* it happens that our culture has become such a frightening environment for some Christians and not for others.[1]

1 Charles Taylor, *A Secular Age* (Cambridge, MA; London: Harvard University Press, 2007), 30. Charles Taylor writes, "What I am trying to describe here is not a theory. Rather my target is our contempo-

THE NEW NORMAL

The culture we live in today began with a new human idea in a beautiful garden. The notion that humankind was free to second-guess its Creator's will gave birth to a firestorm of gut-wrenching and earth-shattering change. Yet, when compared to, say, the latest clothing trends, the rising price of pork bellies, or the final score of yesterday's big game, the firestorm caused by sin has generated relatively little conversation. In fact, the human race has been intent on finding ways either to justify immoral behavior or keep sin under the radar ever since. Trouble is, hiding the fact of sin from one another is hard to do and hiding sin from God is utter foolishness—though that hasn't kept us from trying. The contemporary strategy is to pretend that sin is no longer as damning as it once was.

Historians tell us an extraordinary shift in the psyche of Western culture occurred around 1970. The result has been a prolonged cultural upheaval not seen in almost five hundred years, since Luther's Reformation in AD 1517. Many of God's people (older Christians in particular) have interpreted this roiling turn of events as a diabolical plot to undermine our Christian faith and marginalize biblical ideals. The sheer suddenness of it all has left many of us reeling and bewildered. For our children and grandchildren, however, the radical changes do not seem to be quite as unsettling. It's easy to catch ourselves asking, Why is that?

This cultural shift is also turning out to be an intensely personal matter. It isn't only our government, schools, businesses, entertainment venues, the marketplaces, the communities where we live, or the churches where we worship that have changed. The sobering truth is that we have changed.[2] All of us. Our family's living habits have changed. The way our economy works has changed. How we communicate, think, make decisions—it's all changed. A new normal has embedded itself in our character. Those of us who have been around a little longer struggle to keep up with all the change. Some of us have reached the point of despairing and declared publicly that we hate change because it has done so much to turn our world (and our worldviews) upside down. Yet, the next generation takes them all in stride. We say, "They have acclimated," and then try to move on as best we can.

There is clearly something different in the way young people understand life. What is not clear is the degree to which our changing worldviews are affecting

---

rary lived understanding; that is, the way we naively take things to be. We might say: the construal we just live in, without ever being aware of it as a construal, or—for most of us—without ever even formulating it." (For Taylor's explanation of how the enchanted mind is/was wired, see pp. 29–41.)

2 James K. A. Smith, *How (Not) to Be Secular: Reading Charles Taylor* (Grand Rapids: Eerdmans, 2014), xi. Smith writes, "Taylor's account should also serve as a wake-up call for the church, functioning as a mirror to help us see how we have come to inhabit our secular age. Taylor is not only interested in understanding how 'the secular' emerged; he is also an acute observer of how we're all secular now. The secular touches everything. It not only makes *un*belief possible; it also *changes belief*—it impinges upon Christianity (and all other religious communities)."

us—or them. For example, how have these changing worldviews divided us from one another? It's hard to know. To quote an old saw, "We can't see the forest for the trees." Moreover, living in a sea of unprecedented change makes it hard to distinguish the most strident symptoms of change from their cause.

THE FOG OF BATTLE

When a cultural shift of great magnitude occurs, there is immense, urgent pressure to adopt a new worldview. In the rush, no one has the time to evaluate the crushing effects of change. Meanwhile, the pressure to plow under the soil of our cultural past increases exponentially. It's a double whammy!

Some people are just not able to see what is happening. Some don't want to see it. Some see it and are frozen stiff with fear, unable to react. Then there are those who become angry, without having a clue about why they have a right to be so enraged when they don't even know who the enemy is. (Pick a target; any target will do.)

When a cultural shift of great magnitude occurs, there is immense, urgent pressure to adopt a new worldview.

Lately, the ongoing threat of even more change has given rise to a certain amount of paranoia. One day, we sense hostility from the media. We have our suspicions about every agent being a poser and every agenda being a ruse. We see problems with Hollywood lifestyles, dishonesty on Wall Street, shady White House politics, ineptness in Congress, the shrinking middle class, the rising tide of bureaucracy, a lack of moral education in our nation's public schools, or the outrageous behavior of a celebrity last night on television. Some days, it is just a nagging sensation, like a headache that refuses to subside. On a few rare days, the threat feels definable and immediate. Every once in a while, however, there is a genuine sense that everything is out of whack and the world we live in is profoundly hostile to all that is just, right, and good.

We are, of course, responsible for some of this unpleasantness. Our human drive to be a part of the crowd, to belong, to be current, or just to be relevant is a compelling reason for accepting new norms without examining the ideas that drive them. Or maybe Satan is just more cunning than we credit him. Have we forgotten that when the devil is unsuccessful among the stalwart, he targets the weak, the young, the fragile, the doubting, the vulnerable, the naive and impressionable, picking them off one by one while you and I worry about our losses in the stock market or the most recent health scare? His next victims could be our children or grandchildren. And who of us has never had our own moment of weakness, doubt, or naïveté? We are just as vulnerable as our kids. Besides, as you are about to discover, knowing what Satan is up to is problematic in a culture unwilling to acknowledge that he is real.

IMAGINE A NEW WORLD

Cultures are like people; there is an arc to their life span. In its youth, a budding young culture is full of itself, gorged with idealistic views about how things should be. History tells us there is often a violent struggle when a new culture rises up from the dry bones of its parent. (Consider the transition from Old Testament times to the New Testament era.) Where the ghosts from a distant past still haunt an emergent new worldview, old ideas have to be shaken off—purged—before the new culture can thrive.

The year is 1970—early spring in the life of a fledgling, young culture. Vietnam has been headline news for more than a decade. The national debate about the war has finally been framed as a moral question. Graphic images from the battlefield are broadcast daily into people's living rooms. America is filled with doubt and uncertainty. Its collective worldview is suffering from acute anxiety.

Above the din of massive street protests at home and the carnage in Southeast Asia, a dreamy refrain cuts through the darkness. It touches the hearts of millions, crossing the boundaries of religion, gender, age, race, ethnicity, and politics. It pictures an imagined new world, kinder and gentler than the world people are used to seeing on the evening news. Restless hearts yearn for a unifying alternative. John Lennon is ready to answer the call. He is offering hope, peace, and brotherly love. His confidence is electric: "It's easy if you try." Just imagine. But this Siren's song is an intoxicating call for cultural change that would overturn commonly accepted worldviews that have served as the bulwarks of society for hundreds, if not thousands, of years. Consider what John Lennon wants to throw overboard.

"Imagine"

Imagine there's no Heaven

It's easy if you try

No Hell below us

Above us only sky

Imagine all the people

Living for today . . .

Imagine there's no countries

It isn't hard to do

Nothing to kill or die for

And no religion too

Imagine all the people
Living life in peace . . .
You may say I'm a dreamer
But I'm not the only one
I hope someday you'll join us
And the world will be as one
Imagine no possessions
I wonder if you can
No need for greed or hunger
A brotherhood of man
Imagine all the people
Sharing all the world . . .
You may say I'm a dreamer
But I'm not the only one
I hope someday you'll join us
And the world will live as one.[3]

—John Lennon (1940–80)

Lennon's dream was to usher in a new understanding of the moral life. His vision of the future was anchored to his faith in the goodness of humankind. But like so many others, Lennon believed the rich loam of the existing culture would first need to be plowed under. His strategy was to excavate the soil of religious beliefs and bury biblical truth forever.

Lennon's lyric was just one of the many markers that marshaled in the emergent new worldview. His song was much more a symbol than a cause. Besides, what could be more innocent, or more human, than imagining? Lennon may not have known that his message had a name, but the ideas he espoused were consistent with a godless philosophy known as secular humanism.[4]

---

3 "Imagine" by John Lennon, track 1 on *Imagine*, Apple Records, 1971. See also, AZ Lyrics, accessed January 31, 2017, http://www.azlyrics.com/lyrics/johnlennon/imagine.html.

4 Taylor, *Secular*, 55. Humanism and secularism are two separate schools of thought. Humanism is often associated with the Renaissance movement, which can be traced to Copernicus's discovery that the sun, not the earth, is the center of our solar system (1507). The ideals of secularism are harder to pin down because they vary from one global region to another. The word *secular* comes from the Latin word *saeculum,* "a century or age." Taylor writes, "People who are in the saeculum, are embedded in ordinary time, they are living the life of ordinary time; as against those who have turned away from this in order to live closer to eternity. The word is thus used for ordinary as against higher time. A parallel distinction is temporal/spiritual."

In this book, the word *secular* references the earthly kingdom (secular, temporal). God's heavenly kingdom references a spiritual (transcendent) reality that is completely void of sin or its consequenc-

Secular humanism views the Bible as a collection of ancient artifacts and quaint myths from a bygone era. In a country that once thought of itself as a Christian nation, this anti-biblical worldview now dominates the culture of our present time. For the record, secular humanism has already dominated our culture for several generations.

Secular humanism is America's de facto national religion.

True to form, today's version of secular humanism is a river of ever-changing whims. It is a movement of spiritual notions more than a creed of established doctrines. It includes a fluid menu of random religious ideas borrowed from non-Christian world religions. Its primary contributor, however, is atheism. Today, secular humanism and the pastiche of pagan notions clinging to its unstable frame are forming the character of the overwhelming majority of our nation's youth. Secular humanism is America's de facto national religion. Moreover, it is the elusive force behind the pressure to rid ourselves of biblical truth and Reformation values.[5] It prospers under the assumption that former narratives are obsolete. Its proponents continue to assert that the world cannot be completely transformed until we have abandoned all the biblical foolishness of the past. The momentum for achieving this cultural transformation has been surging for centuries. The society in which we live today is no longer the shared foundation of biblical worldviews it once was. Charles Taylor writes:

> We no longer live in societies in which the widespread sense can be maintained that faith in God is central to the ordered life we (partially) enjoy. It is a pluralistic world, in which many forms of belief and unbelief jostle, and hence fragilize each other. It is a world in which belief has lost many of the social matrices which made it seem "obvious" and "unchallengeable."[6]

Lennon's poetry triggered a magical mystery tour in America's collective imagination. No one can pinpoint the exact moment when the actual event occurred. The Western world finally reached the tipping point within a few months or years

---

es. This kingdom is timeless (eternal). Both humanism and secularism are based on the sin-tainted notion that man is the measure of all things. A basic tenet of secular humanism is that human beings are capable of being moral people without being religious; that is, without acknowledging or worshiping God, or god(s). A biblical worldview categorically rejects this godless belief.

5 Taylor, *Secular*, 530. "We can ask: what stopped people (that is, almost everybody) from being able to adopt stances of unbelief in 1500? One answer is the enchanted world; in a cosmos of spirits and forces, some of them evil and destructive, one had to hold on to whatever was conceived to be the mainstay of good power, our bulwark against evil. Another answer was: that belief was so interwoven with social life that one was hardly conceivable without the other."

6 Taylor, *Secular*, 531.

on either side of the release of Lennon's song. A cultural shift that rivaled the narratives of every other major cultural shift in world history was underway. Its primary effect was that people were now liberated to imagine their world without God.

THE REFORMATION ERA

The culture that had dominated the Western world before 1970 spanned almost five hundred years. If the date that marks the tipping point is set at 1970, only one-fifth of today's population in America lived during the final life stage of the five-hundred-year culture that had been framed by the Lutheran Reformation.[7] Historians call it "The Reformation Era."[8] For almost five centuries, the ideas conceived by Luther's Reformation influenced the cultures of Western Europe. During these five centuries, most people could not have imagined their world without God.

While it was drawn from the foundational culture of the Early Christian Church, medieval biases about the Bible's teachings had developed a false image of God, making Him appear to be a cruel judge, whose justice threatened one's soul without mercy. In this climate, the consciences of God's people were shackled by legalism, stifling superstition, and heretical promises that held up good works as the means for appeasing God's vengeful anger. Luther's Reformation provided a whole new understanding of moral living and the relationship between human beings and their Creator. His emphasis on God's grace, as opposed to the Roman Church's emphasis on works-righteousness, put an end to people's hopeless bondage to the Law.

Luther's Reformation provided a whole new understanding of moral living and the relationship between human beings and their Creator.

This is not to say that everyone who lived during these five centuries, and within the vast geographic regions of Western Europe and the New World, were all Christians. But it does speak to how the Reformation shaped the worldviews of millions. Luther not only reformed God's church on earth, but he also changed virtually all of Western culture. People were now psychologically hardwired to a cultural frame that came directly from God's Word and focused specifically on the

7 US Census Bureau, America's Population Distribution by Age, 2010.

8 We have steadfastly resisted using the term "Post-Reformation Era" because, in our opinion, Luther's ideas continue to inform and reform God's people, the Church. They will continue to do so until Christ returns in judgment.

threefold truths of faith alone, divine grace alone, and the revelation of inspired Scripture alone.

Culturally, the Reformation touched every aspect of life. Luther's concepts of vocation and the priesthood of all believers gave the lives of ordinary people new meaning and purpose. Family life was redefined. Formal education rose to a much higher level in the hierarchy of values. The ideas that drive modern science today had their beginnings in the Reformation and led to the dismantling of false, medieval presuppositions. Life began, was lived, and finally ended with rites and rituals shaped by Reformation ideals that were, in turn, rooted in Scripture. But Reformation ideals also gave rise to radical political worldviews regarding earthly authority, which frequently led to radical and violent new ideas about governance and national identities.

The Reformation worldview was inescapable. In a cultural sense, it was equally inescapable for believers and unbelievers—until one biblical concept that had been universally accepted was lost. It was the loss of this single, critical idea that served as the impetus for the major cultural shift that finally rocked the world around 1970.

Now, for optimistic Christians, hearing that the ideals of Luther's Reformation once permeated Western culture, and that it lasted for almost five hundred years, sounds like a huge advancement in world history. In some ways, it surely was that. Having God at the center of one's culture, as well as the Lord of the church, certainly made life a lot easier. But there was an unintended consequence accompanying this phenomenon. Because it had become a part of the common worldview, the Christian community (the church) relaxed its stress on teaching a quintessential Bible assumption we will refer to as *transcendency*. Transcendency was the critical Bible truth that was lost.

ANOTHER KINGDOM

Transcendency is actually a scriptural understanding of a second (but certainly not secondary) reality. Transcendent reality is unlike the physical realities of our existence in this life on earth. God lives in His own transcendent reality. It is His timeless, spaceless, changeless spiritual domain—a domain that, in divine love, He freely gives to those who trust in His promises. Because the idea of a transcendent kingdom had become so fully embedded in the popular culture's worldview, people who did not believe in Jesus as their Savior were still likely to believe in transcendent concepts such as heaven and hell, miracles, the devil and his demons, prayer, even the concept of a divine being. If the biblical teaching of God's transcendent kingdom had continued to be construed as one of the primary teachings of the Christian church, things might have been quite different. But

God's people had become spiritually lazy. Letting culture do the church's work of preaching God's spiritual kingdom turned out to be the coup that changed everything around 1970. And perhaps the real moral lesson here is this: *When the Bible's teachings are framed as cultural values or social imperatives, instead of being framed as divine truth, they lose their moral authority.*

Without using the word *transcendent*, Jesus taught His followers about the transcendent kingdom of God. He referred to this spiritual reality as either "the kingdom of God" or "the kingdom of heaven." Many of Jesus' kingdom parables contrasted our earthly lives with the eternal reality of God's domain.

The kingdom of God is just as real as our physical existence, though our human senses (seeing, hearing, touching, tasting, smelling) are of little help in proving it exists. God's kingdom cannot be measured, studied, or understood in the same way that our earthly reality can be examined. It is spiritual. God's kingdom is extraordinary, or perhaps "trans-ordinary." It is a reality all its own. We are hard-pressed to define or describe this divine kingdom beyond what Scripture tells us. Yet, we can say with confidence, we are already experiencing it in a limited way in the here and now of this life. Paul says, "For the kingdom of God is not a matter of eating and drinking but of righteousness and peace and joy in the Holy Spirit. Whoever thus serves Christ is acceptable to God and approved by men" (Romans 14:17–18).

The first few words of the Bible assert that God's reality is different from the reality we know in our earthly existence. From the very onset of His divine narrative, we are made aware that God transcends everything. Consider the impact of the Bible's opening line: "In the beginning, God . . ." (Genesis 1:1). Those first four words carry a lot of weight. Everything that follows—all sixty-six of the Bible's books—are firmly anchored in these words. They tell us that the reality of God is not up for debate. On this score, nothing more needs to be said. His universal presence is to be assumed. This is His book, written by His handpicked, inspired authors. If someone wishes to debate the God question, they will have to go somewhere else to find resources of questionable human authority, reputation, integrity, and motives. Here, in these sacred pages, His transcendent authority rests supreme over all things. God *is*. Everything else is created.

This is how God wants to present Himself to believers and unbelievers. We hear it and believe it with the conviction that a good and righteous God would not—could not—lie to us. It is an article of faith. People may refuse to believe it, or they can lose their faith and stop believing it, but nothing can invalidate God's Word.[9] Long after our planet is gone, this truth will still be standing.

9 See 2 Samuel 7:28; Psalm 146:6; Romans 3:4; Hebrews 6:18.

In his book *A Secular Age*, Charles Taylor uses the word *enchanted* to describe God's kingdom. However unfortunate, words such as *enchanted*, or even *disenchantment*, sound more like the make-believe fantasy of childhood than the promise of eternal life in the new heavens and the new earth. Yet, what one receives in Baptism and through faith transcends the reality of our physical world. In that sense, the enchanted glory, which none of us has a right to hope for, is ours just for the believing. What Taylor means is that life in God's kingdom has an enchanted quality to everything about it—an impossible dream that is, against all odds, a full and complete reality. Taylor is using it in contrast to the word *disenchantment*, a word that appears frequently in contemporary literature to describe the godless cultural worldview that dominates our age. "Disenchanted" correctly defines a culture in which the biblical concept of transcendency has been forgotten, ignored, or dismissed outright.[10] "Disenchanted" correctly defines our culture's present, dominant worldview of all human reality.

Having a transcendent God and living with a two-kingdom worldview is a critical component of our faith life and crucial to the formation of Christian character. Without a two-kingdom worldview, human character is just plain character.

A GODLESS ALTERNATIVE

By the early 1800s, the popular culture that had been radically transformed by Luther's Reformation was beginning to show its age. The erosion was slow at first. In particular, those who believed that it was possible to create heaven on earth by embedding biblical ideas in an earthly culture were disappointed. Many were already searching for alternatives.

Then, in 1859, a British naturalist named Charles Darwin published a book that proposed a new theory to explain how human life began. Darwin's *On the Origin of the Species* offered an alternative to the divinely inspired account Moses provided in Genesis 1. Darwin directly challenged the biblical concept of transcendency, arguing that human life was the accidental product of an evolutionary process known as natural selection.[11] The book caught the attention of people looking for an alternative to Scripture's account of a six-day creation by divine

10 Taylor, *Secular*, 25–26. Regarding his use of the terms *enchanted* and *disenchanted*, Taylor explains, "This is perhaps not the best expression; it seems to evoke light and fairies. But I am invoking here its negation, Weber's expression of 'disenchantment' as a description of our modern condition. This term has achieved such wide currency in our discussion of these matters, that I am going to use its antonym to describe a crucial feature of the pre-modern condition. The enchanted world in this sense is the world of spirits, demons, and moral forces which our ancestors lived in."

11 We do not have a theological issue with the mechanism of natural selection itself. Natural selection can be observed. The theological issue with Darwin is the claim that we have a natural origin without requiring God, which is clearly counter to what God tells us in His inspired Scriptures: "In the beginning, God created" (Genesis 1:1).

fiat. With the influence of this new worldview growing rapidly, and confidence in Reformation thought ebbing, science was poised to become the tip of the spear for the dawning of a new era.

Over the next century, Darwin's theory rose to prominence. By the 1960s, many young people in America accepted evolution as a mainstream belief. Secular universities defended the theory of evolution with such zeal that it was no longer taught as theory, but was instead accepted as indisputable scientific fact.

Darwin's explanation for the origin of human life was so widely accepted that some Christian denominations tried to harmonize the Bible's creation account with evolutionary theory. Others tried to mythologize the six-day Genesis account.[12] These attempts cast a dark shadow on Scripture's preeminence as the only source of absolute truth. In cultural terms, science was beginning to be accepted as the secular equivalent to the truth of God's inspired Word.[13] Culture no longer stood in the way of exercising the godless option. People had an alternative to the Bible's explanation for the origin of life. In time, they would also have the cultural alternative to explain life itself without any need to see God as life's author.

The crux of the matter was, and still is, truth. Common sense tells us that either a thing is true or it isn't.[14] When the intrinsic value of truth is diminished, it is automatically disqualified as valid. But, in an egalitarian society, where culture is often shaped by the tension between a secular worldview and a religious worldview, compromise is the inevitable strategy for dealing with all conflicts concerning truth. In the environment of compromise, biblical truth always becomes something less than essential truth.

The Scopes "Monkey" Trial, which took place in the small town of Dayton, Tennessee, in 1925, was an effort to resolve the cultural tension between biblical

---

12 Lange, *God So Loved*, 151. Lange writes, "The whole Bible, then, accepts the Genesis account of creation as historical fact. To interpret it in any other way is to ignore the context of Genesis itself, the witness of the rest of the Bible and the testimony of Christ and his apostles (to whom he promised the gift of inspiration). It is only when people approach the Genesis account of creation with a biased mind that they can try to harmonize creation and evolution. If a person looks carefully at the context of Genesis and the testimony of the rest of the Bible, he or she cannot arrive at the view that the creation account is a myth."

13 Smith, *(Not) to Be Secular*, viii. Smith writes, "Your neighbors inhabit what Charles Taylor calls an 'immanent frame'; they are no longer bothered by 'the God question' *as* a question because they are devotees of 'exclusive humanism'—a way of being in-the-world that offers significance without transcendence. They don't feel like anything is missing."

14 Smith, *(Not) to Be Secular,* 100. Smith quotes Taylor, making this point: "What's at stake in this invocation of 'science' is less an account of empirical data and more an 'ethic,' a stance taken with respect to the world. 'The convert to the new ethics has learned to mistrust some of his own deepest instincts, and in particular those which draw him to religious belief. . . . The crucial change is in the status accorded to the inclination to believe; this is the object of a radical shift in interpretation. It is no longer the impetus in us towards truth, but has become rather the most dangerous temptation to sin against the austere principles of belief formation.'"

truth and scientific truth.[15] Whether it was an intended outcome or not, this case changed worldviews about the sources, nature, and substance of truth.

The Scopes Trial was supposed to be a test case for the Butler Act, a Tennessee law that prohibited public school teachers from denying the biblical account of life's origin. The same law also made it unlawful to teach human evolution from animal ancestry in state-funded schools. The trial was a media circus. Staged to attract publicity, both sides saw an advantage in trying to win the support of popular opinion. Two of the nation's leading lawyers, William Jennings Bryan (prosecution), a Christian fundamentalist, and Clarence Darrow (defense), an avowed agnostic, squared off. The case was seen as a theological contest between Modernists, who claimed evolution was not inconsistent with religion, and Fundamentalists, who said the words of God, as revealed in the Bible, took priority over all human knowledge. John Scopes, a high school biology teacher, was tried, found guilty, and fined one hundred dollars. The verdict was later overturned on a technicality.[16]

The trial settled nothing. The law in question was not repealed until 1967. Darwin's theory had finally garnered enough popular support to become our culture's accepted explanation for the origin of human life. Culturally speaking, God was no longer a necessary factor in determining how life began.

The Scopes Trial is important to our conversation for several reasons. First, this historical event shows that science had finally achieved a kind of parity with divinely inspired, biblical truth. The God question could now be debated on the basis of science in a variety of high-profile venues. Second, the Scopes Trial demonstrated that civil law could be used to limit or remove established religious convictions from the public square. Third, the democratic premise of majority rules had been so thoroughly embedded in the American psyche that the majority opinion was now commonly being interpreted as a source and in some cases the only source for moral truth. The practical effect on society was that the ambiguous and ever-changing ethical positions taken by secular humanism could survive public scrutiny as a legitimate cultural worldview. This is especially important for our conversation because it was popular opinion that eventually drove American education to its current ethical position in public schools. But if the criterion for judging ethical action is the contemporaneous, collective conscience, there is no valid standard, since the common conscience is constantly mutating.[17]

---

15 Douglas O. Linder, "State v. John Scopes ('The Monkey Trial'): An Account," Famous Trials, accessed May 29, 2017, http://www.famous-trials.com/scopesmonkey/2127-home.

16 Linder, "State v. John Scopes."

17 John Warwick Montgomery, *The Law above the Law: Why the Law Needs Biblical Foundations; How Legal Thought Supports Christian Truth* (Irvine: CA: NRP Books, 1975), 21. The prodigious author and lecturer writes, "When public morals decay and the times degenerate, of what consequence is so-

In today's moral climate, we have a plentiful menu of truth sources from which to choose. Our moral worldviews are free to select any of four sources for truth to suit any given circumstance. Small wonder that some historians have taken to calling our current age the Post-Truth Era. Ironically, some Christians tend to be enthusiastic about the choices this smorgasbord provides. And, to be truthful, none of the three pretenders is inherently evil. In pragmatic terms, all three have occasionally proven helpful in resolving some of history's more difficult social conundrums. But what is important here is that none of the three pretenders can lay claim to representing the absolute truth of a good, just, and loving God, who has demonstrated His total commitment to sacrificing His kingdom and His life to redeem His fallen creatures.

In a culture of moral ambiguities, God's pure and holy truth stands above all human forms of the truth.

Only one of these four claimants for being the "absolute truth" is truly absolute. Social opinions are fickle. Science is periodically forced to accept new findings. The first seven decades under the rule of the American Constitution were spent languishing under the moral burden of legalized slavery. In a culture of moral ambiguities, God's pure and holy truth stands above all human forms of the truth. It is, quite literally, "the truth, the whole truth, and nothing but the truth."

IN THE DOCK

In the same year that John Lennon released "Imagine," and just three years after the repeal of the Butler Act, a collection of essays by the brilliant British scholar and popular author C. S. Lewis was released. In one of the essays, Lewis made this chilling observation:

> The ancient man approached God (or even the gods) as the accused person approaches his judge. For the modern man, the roles are quite reversed. [Man] is the judge: God is in the dock. [Man] is quite a kindly judge; if God should have a reasonable defense for being the god who permits war, poverty and disease, [man] is ready to listen to it. The trial may even end in God's acquittal. But the important thing is that Man is on the bench and God is in the Dock.[18]

ciety's approval or reputation for ethical action? If all Cretans are liars, is it a compliment to be praised by a Cretan? And in such a situation, what is the individual or collective conscience necessarily worth? Conscience is environmentally conditioned, and the morals of the time will influence what is regarded as conscionable or unconscionable. Among cannibals, one feels guilty for not cleaning his plate."

18 C. S. Lewis, "God in the Dock," *God in the Dock: Essays on Theology and Ethics,* ed. Walter Hooper (Grand Rapids: Eerdmans, 1970), 244.

Lewis understood that natural man believes he can achieve his destiny without divine intervention. Lewis also knew that an ancient Jewish court had placed the Son of God in the dock, found Him guilty on bogus charges, and forced His unjust execution. God has been in the dock before. For the unbelieving world, He has always been in the dock. In a changing world that was still reeling from the horrors of World War II, Lewis felt compelled to sound the alarm of yet another area of our biblical faith that was under attack.

By the 1960s, some of humankind's most important institutions were on the rocks. Marriage, for one. Families, for another. Racial relationships were already in triage. But the relationships under the greatest duress were those relationships that involved respect for authority. Young people were generally encouraged to challenge authority. Some learned to dismiss, disregard, rebel against, or dishonor the authority of parents, teachers, and law enforcement. Some sought to undermine the authority of our government. The erosion has continued to eat away at the fabric of American morality ever since.

In the environment of deteriorating authority, it is not hard to imagine a culture in which the authority of our divine Judge could also be understood as arbitrary. God's image as the Judge of His created universe was compromised and eventually reduced to that of a toothless, cuddly, old grandfatherly figure. It was only a matter of time until the tables had finally turned and humankind sat on the bench, with God in the dock.

But now hear, O Jacob My servant,
Israel whom I have chosen!
Thus says the LORD *who made you,*
who formed you from the womb
and will help you:
Fear not, O Jacob My servant,
Jeshurun whom I have chosen.
For I will pour water on the thirsty land,
and streams on the dry ground;
I will pour My Spirit upon your offspring,
and My blessing on your descendants.

—Isaiah 44:1–3

CHAPTER 5

A Model for All Time

If godly character is the objective, the active participation of God's Spirit in the formation of character is quintessential. He is in the business of transforming character. The Old Testament patriarch Jacob is one of His great character-reclamation projects. Jacob's life brings to mind a number of character-formation issues plaguing our culture today. We can learn a lot about ourselves by studying his life.[1]

THE CONTENDERS

Rebekah's pregnancy was agonizing. Day and night, the jostling in her belly became so violent, she finally asked God to help her understand why her unborn child was struggling.

God's response must have been perplexing: "Two nations are in your womb, and two peoples from within you shall be divided; the one shall be stronger than the other, and the older shall serve the younger" (Genesis 25:23).[2]

As it happened, Esau, the "Hairy One," breached first. But as the twins exited their mother's birth canal, the second infant gripped his older brother's heel. This strange push to daylight was apparently welcomed as an explanation for God's riddle. The boys' father, Isaac, named his second son Jacob, which means

1 The narrative of Jacob's life fills almost half of the Book of Genesis (chs. 25–49).

2 Paul E. Kretzmann, *Old Testament*, vol. 1, Popular Commentary of the Bible (St. Louis: Concordia Publishing House, 1923), 57. Kretzmann's interpretation of the Lord's answer to Rebekah's question recognizes that these words prophetically indicate that Jacob, the younger twin, "would be the bearer and heir of the Messianic promise."

"Heel-grabber." The Hebrew word can also be translated "he deceives" or just "deceiver." The label was well suited to the boy's disposition. In Scripture, as in life, names matter.

We need God more than we need air to breathe. But for young Jacob, from what we can tell from Scripture, life was not about needing God or even wanting God in his life. Jacob's worldview was all about self. In a word, he was self-centered. He probably was also unbearably self-indulgent, self-reliant, self-consumed, self-delusional, and self-infatuated. At its heart, this was, of course, self-idolatry. Jacob's worldview served his ego and curried to his will. And if he couldn't get his selfish heart's desire in an ethical way, Jacob was capable of getting what he wanted by taking matters into his own hands, even if that meant doing something immoral.

In young Jacob, we get a snapshot of how God's template for human character is spoiled by sin. Jacob believed he could have whatever he wanted, either because he was entitled to it or because he was so clever. Consequently, Jacob refused to be held accountable for the way he conducted his life. And while we are historically quite removed from Jacob's circumstances, the age we live in has many of the same attitudes embedded in this worldview. We live in a narcissistic culture in which the self craves all of the attention.

We should be careful not to use the narrative of Jacob's life to indict his father and mother. We know that Jacob's parents were reverent and sincere believers in God's promises. We can imagine them teaching their children about the God of creation, the God of the great flood, the God of the promise, and the God of Noah and Abraham. As can be seen in the case of our first parents' heartbreaking experience in raising their first son, Cain (Genesis 4), it does happen that godly parents, who have the very best of intentions, are unable to lead a stubborn and lost child to the sanctuary of God's love. This is one of the most agonizing consequences of sin—a painful aspect of the Christian life of cross-bearing. While it would hardly have been much consolation, Jacob's parents needed to know that it was Jacob's choice. Though they undoubtedly had their faults and fights and were far from perfect, nothing they could have said or done would have been able to change the fact that at this particular time in his life, Jacob just didn't care. We can surmise that at this point in his life, the god he secretly worshiped was himself. He lacked humility. He was blind to his own self-centered character and would not have been able to understand that he was his own worst enemy.

THE BARTERED BLESSING

In the ancient cultures of the Middle East, the oldest son was the heir apparent to the family birthright. The birthright generally included property, wealth, livestock, and the right to conduct family business. In the case of Jacob's family, there were added implications. The birthright that Isaac would pass on to his first-born male heir included a covenant that God had promised to the twins' paternal grandfather. In that multilayered promise, God told Abraham, "I will make of you a great nation, and I will bless you and make your name great, so that you will be a blessing. I will bless those who bless you, and him who dishonors you I will curse, and in you all the families of the earth shall be blessed" (Genesis 12:2–3).

Did you note how often God referenced blessings in His promise? It was an itemized extension of the very first blessing that flowed from God's loving heart when He created Adam and Eve. Some aspects of this more detailed promise can be interpreted as physical blessings, while others were psychological or social. But on the whole, God's cluster of promises had a much deeper significance regarding life in His transcendent kingdom.[3]

Abraham trusted God at His Word and passed these promises on to his son Isaac. Isaac, in turn, planned to pass the same wonderful promise on to his eldest son, Esau, as part of the family birthright.

And who wouldn't be delighted to inherit such an extraordinary prize?

Well, brother Esau apparently didn't see much value in it. Unlike the homebody that Jacob was, Esau busied himself with the life of a vagabond. Based on what we know from Scripture, it's not hard to imagine that he would disappear into the wilderness for weeks, free from the meddling eyes of family members, free to pursue his own wild pleasures. Esau's untamed worldview saw family history as irrelevant and family traditions as trivial. It's likely that the promise of a Messiah meant little to him.

One day, Esau returned home after a long, unsuccessful hunt. He was famished. The first person he met was Jacob, who just happened to be cooking a pot of stew. Always the opportunist, Jacob offered his twin brother a taste. That was followed by an offer Esau couldn't refuse—a bowl of savory soup in exchange for the family birthright.

Esau wasn't starving to death; he was just very hungry. Nor did he have the right to trade away the birthright. Scripture bluntly asserts that Esau despised his birthright. At the same time, it would only be fair to ask if Jacob negotiated this unusual exchange with a clear conscience and in an altruistic spirit. We are better off letting God decide the moral implications of this transaction. What we can say is that, at least in principle, the birthright now belonged to Jacob.

3 The fulfillment of the messianic portion of God's promise to Abraham is later confirmed in Acts 3:25–26 and Galatians 3:8–9.

THE MASK

When Jacob and Esau were about 40 years old, and their father had reached the old age of 137, the time for Isaac to pass the birthright on to Esau had finally arrived. Apparently, no one had ever bothered to mention to old Isaac that his eldest son had bartered the family's birthright-blessing away to Jacob for a pot of soup. With God's prophetic words still echoing in her ears, Rebekah conspired with Jacob to deceive her elderly husband into giving the inheritance to Jacob, the heel-grabber. Maybe Rebekah felt God needed her help. More likely, she hated Esau's two Hittite wives so much that she was willing to accept responsibility for what was about to happen.

The strategy was to conceal Jacob's true identity from his father. This time, Jacob's behavior clearly was immoral. He knew that what he was doing was wrong.

Sinners—believers and unbelievers alike—are quite adept at hiding their true identity from other people. There are times when we don't want anyone to know what's going on in our minds or hearts. After Adam and Eve committed the first sin, God gave them animal skins to cover their disgrace and increase their sense of shame. Those animal skins were history's first recorded masks. One day people would look back at those first items of human clothing and see God foreshadowing Jesus' robe of righteousness, given to sinful humankind to cover our guilt with God's own goodness. Since the first sin, though, the whole human race has become skillful at masking our sinful intentions. We hide our arrogance as we stand in judgment over those who seem less righteous than we think we are. We cover our loveless behaviors and disguise our selfish greed as we plan to take more than our fair share. We conceal our hateful anger and private longings as we plot to abuse the bodies, human rights, or self-esteem of others. We camouflage our corrupt business dealings with backslaps, handshakes, and flattery. The brutal truth is that we are so committed to covering up our sinful condition that it would be impossible to have a meaningful conversation about human character without giving due consideration to the masks we wear and the ways we wear them.

Isaac's eyesight was weak, but he might still know if this was truly Esau by the gamey odor of his son's hunting duds. So, Jacob donned Esau's rank hunting clothes. Rebekah cooked a pot of lamb stew, filling the tent with the succulent aroma of Esau's secret ingredients. Jacob thought of his brother's hairy body. What if old Isaac embraced him? So, Rebekah stitched lambskins together to mask Jacob's hairless arms and neck.

The deception worked, until Isaac asked if the son kneeling before him was really Esau. Faced with being exposed as a deceiver, Jacob lied.

Isaac believed the lie and passed the family blessing on to the heel-grabber. If he knew that Jacob was deceiving him, perhaps old Isaac was remembering that

Jacob was God's choice for receiving the family birthright, even before the twins were born.

Esau, on the other hand, was so enraged by Jacob's treachery that he vowed to kill his twin just as soon as their father was in the grave.

With Esau's death threat dangling like Damocles's sword over Jacob's head, Rebekah helped Jacob flee to the safety of her brother's home in Mesopotamia (modern-day Iraq and other areas). Jacob would remain there in exile for the next twenty years.

THE HEAVENLY STAIRCASE

On one of the first nights of his journey, Jacob camped using a stone for his pillow. There he had a vision in which he saw God standing at the top of a tiered structure that rested on the desert floor. The towering edifice was impressive. It reached far into the night sky, as though its majestic terraced staircase would lead to the very gates of heaven. Angels promenaded up and down the tiers that connected earth and heaven. They ministered to Jacob, lifting his spirit and restoring his strength.

Suddenly, the Lord spoke. What He said thrilled Jacob. God promised to help Jacob return to his home in Canaan. Alone and uncertain of his future, Jacob was comforted. Then God repeated the same promise He had made two generations earlier to Jacob's grandfather Abraham—God promised to send a Savior from sin's curse through the family bloodline, a homeland of his own, blessings for his friendly neighbors, and the promise to protect him from his enemies. God did not want Jacob to doubt for a minute that the blessing he had stolen from Esau was his. While God did not approve of Jacob's intervening efforts to make it his own, He wanted Jacob to know that this legacy had always been promised to him in eternity.

When Jacob awoke, he knew he had spent the night in God's presence. In light of what had just happened with his family, it is easy to imagine in this moment how he shamefully thought of the terrible way he had treated his father and Esau. It may well have been the first time in his life that Jacob thought seriously about his relationship with God. It is likely that he remembered the lessons about God from his father and mother.

Jacob bowed to the God of his father and grandfather. Then he commended his life to the God of that transcendent promise and consecrated the place where he had slept. It was a solemn moment. He wanted to memorialize the spot where he had met God. Pouring oil on the stone he had used as his pillow, Jacob named the place Bethel, which means "house of God." Twenty years later, the Lord would send angels to lead him back home to another remarkable encounter with the God who loved him and wanted only to bless him.

A SELF-MADE MAN

While the lion's share of any individual's formation occurs early in life, godly character develops over a lifetime.

This point bears repeating: While the lion's share of any individual's formation occurs early in life, godly character develops over a lifetime. At age 40, Jacob's dreamlike encounter with God was just the beginning. Over the next twenty years, his life would be plagued by adversity and challenge. God would use this unsettling time in Jacob's life to serve an eternal purpose—another blessing, even if Jacob could not have acknowledged its goodness.[4]

Uncle Laban turned out to be just as shrewd as Jacob. Now, Laban had two unmarried daughters, both single and of marrying age. Their names were Rachel and Leah. Rachel was beautiful; Leah was not. Jacob fell in love with the younger daughter, Rachel. When Jacob asked his Uncle Laban for Rachel's hand in exchange for seven years of labor, his devious uncle hatched a bait-and-switch scam that tricked Jacob into marrying her sister Leah. Still in love with Rachel, Jacob offered to work seven more years for Rachel's hand. Laban quickly agreed.

The plural marriage between Jacob and these two sisters was a recipe for disaster. Both wanted to please their husband by producing as many male heirs as possible. They were jealous of each other, and their fiercely competitive personalities often led them to be mean and petty. Each time one of them was having difficulty in getting pregnant, she would insist that Jacob use her handmaiden as a surrogate partner to conceive another child. Both sisters played the same game. The result was more sons for Jacob—twelve in all. With a growing family came even more domestic conflict.

Jacob's relationship with his Uncle Laban fared no better. Sometime during his twenty years in Laban's employ, Jacob perfected a way to predict, and perhaps even promote, the birth of dark-colored lambs and spotted or speckled goats. Jacob convinced Laban to let him cull the oddly marked lambs and goats to begin a modest flock of his own. Such animals were generally rare, so Laban did not feel threatened. But Jacob's flocks and herds began to grow quickly, while Laban's dwindled. Soon, there were more speckled baby goats and dark lambs than

4 The events of Jacob's life show us how God works good for His people and on behalf of His kingdom. (See Romans 8:28.)

light-colored animals. Jacob became a wealthy man. Laban stewed over his own bad luck.

After twenty years of infighting, Jacob had enough. He wanted to go home.

THE STRANGER

The overland journey home was tedious. As Jacob's caravan approached Canaan, he sent emissaries ahead to learn what they could about Esau's whereabouts. Their instructions were to tell Esau that Jacob was sorry for treating him so poorly twenty years earlier. Jacob wanted to make amends.

When the scouts returned, they reported that Esau and a crowd of four hundred men were headed straight for Jacob's caravan.

Always resourceful, Jacob sent several herds and flocks of livestock ahead—goats, sheep, camels, donkeys. He wanted to placate Esau. Then Jacob ordered his men to disperse the animals over the desert floor. Finally, Jacob divided his people into two groups and sent them across the river, instructing the groups to travel in opposite directions. His thinking was likely that if Esau attacked him, perhaps half might escape while the other group was being annihilated. Then, Jacob found himself alone on the banks of the River Jabbok. He prayed, asking God to deliver him, petitioning the Lord to bless his offspring, as God had promised.

Without warning, Jacob was suddenly attacked. (Read about it in Genesis 32.) At first, he may have thought it was Esau, avenging his honor. But Jacob didn't recognize the man. (Scripture does not identify the assailant by name.) The attacker rushed in from the darkness, seeking Jacob. The two engaged in hand-to-hand combat.

Two points need to be made about this attack. The first has to do with the assailant's identity. The place where Jacob camped no doubt rekindled memories of that night twenty years earlier, when God made those wonderful promises to him. Somehow, Jacob seems to have sensed that this event was one of those rare moments of opportunity that he needed to seize. He probably even began to suspect that his attacker was God Himself, masking his divine identity.[5] Remember, Jacob's first encounter with God happened while he was in a dream state. This second event was happening in real time and in an actual place. During the first encounter, Jacob had witnessed God's glory and majesty, but only as a vision.

5 Werner H. Franzmann, *Old Testament*, Bible History Commentary. WELS Board for Parish Education (Milwaukee: Northwestern Publishing House, 1980), 168. Franzmann writes, "We know that this was more than a man. In Hosea 12:4, 5, Jacob's opponent is termed 'the angel.' Here again we encounter the Second Person of the Godhead, the Christ. . . . What is this? God cannot overpower a mere man? As the God of omnipotent power he must always prevail, of course. But as the God of grace he is 'weak' in the face of the believers' prayers, and they will prevail with him." (See 2 Corinthians 12:10.)

Jacob's second encounter with God was down and dirty, physically violent to the point of being deeply unsettling.

But why the disguise? Why would God want to conceal His identity from Jacob?

The practice of masking did not originate with humans. God invented it. There are other examples in both the Old Testament and the New Testament when God masks Himself to conceal His own identity.[6] Siegbert W. Becker explains:

> God does not hide himself because he wants to remain undiscovered and unknown to us. In a sermon which he preached in Wittenberg early in 1517, [Luther] said, "A man hides what he is in order to deny it; God hides what he is in order to reveal it. . . . God in his mercy hides from us that which would destroy us if we were to gaze at it. Nevertheless God wants us to know him. This," Luther says, "is clear from his command that his Word should be preached in all the world to all creatures."[7]

A second point has to do with the suddenness of the Stranger's attack. Using the element of surprise is always a good tactic for getting the drop on an opponent. God sometimes uses this strategy to grab our attention and catch us off guard. C. S. Lewis writes:

> It is always shocking to meet life where we thought we were alone. "Look out!" we cry, "it's *alive*." And therefore this is the very point at which so many draw back—I would have done so myself if I could—and proceed no further with Christianity. An "impersonal God"—well and good. A subjective God of beauty, truth and goodness, inside our own heads—better still. A formless life-force surging through us, a vast power which we can tap—best of all. But God Himself, alive, pulling at the other end of the cord, perhaps approaching at an infinite speed, the hunter, king, husband—that is quite another matter. There comes a moment when the children who have been playing at burglars hush suddenly: was that a *real* footstep in the hall? There comes a moment when people who have been dabbling in religion ("Man's search for God!") suddenly draw back. Supposing we really found Him? We never meant it to come to *that*! Worse still, supposing He found us?[8]

---

6 See Acts 17:27 and Isaiah 55:6.

7 Becker, *Foolishness*, 16–17.

8 C. S. Lewis, *A Year with C. S. Lewis: Daily Readings from His Classic Works* (New York: HarperCollins,

The Stranger's bull rush must have frightened Jacob half to death. God in the flesh! He has come into Jacob's camp in holy love, seeking His dear child, wanting to get his full attention, but certainly not to crush him. The gifts he brings come without warning—unearned, undeserved, and completely unexpected. No sinner has the right to anticipate God's grace, yet we wait with complete confidence because He is always faithful. His blessings appear new each day on the doorstep of our lives—fresh and vibrant, always thrilling, a breathtaking surprise—the surprise of a lifetime.[9]

THE TEST

Jacob must have wondered where he was getting the physical endurance to continue his fight with the Stranger. He seemed to understand there was something about this wrestling match worth pursuing. A blessing, perhaps. But how deep would Jacob have to dig to find the strength to take God down? The answer would come soon enough and be abundantly clear. The Stranger had been providing the strength so that Jacob could continue to engage Him all the more.[10]

Few human activities are more intimate than hand-to-hand combat. If you have ever wrestled with another person—really wrestled—you would remember all the physical contact that goes on. You would also recall the challenging positions, the takedowns, the reversals, and the hand-fighting, not to mention the pain of bruised bones, aching muscles, and tortured tendons. Wrestling can be unpleasant, with the sweat, the constant pushing and pulling, the snapping and lifting. But it can also be exhilarating.

Without question, wrestling with God is a test of faith. But it is not an aspect of faith life that comes naturally.

God wants to enjoy spiritual intimacy with us. He invites us to touch His heart with our prayers.[11] He is eager to have us restrain Him in our moments of crisis. He urges us to cling to Him in faith. He wants us to do everything in our power to keep Him in our feeble grasp. At the same time, He wants to touch us with His love, drawing us ever closer to Himself with the power of His Word. None of this can happen if we flee from His loving embrace. These wrestling matches with God are never intended to force us to bow to God in loving adoration; they are intend-

2003), 3.

9 See Lamentations 3:22–23.

10 Jacob knew the story about the day when, in obedience to God's command, his grandfather Abraham was about to sacrifice Abraham's son Isaac. The angel of the Lord intervened, providing a ram as a substitute. Abraham called the place "The Lord will provide." (See Genesis 22:1–14.)

11 See Isaiah 55:6 and Matthew 7:7–9.

ed to bring His love into our camp to show us how committed He is to keeping His promises of forgiveness and redemption.

Without question, wrestling with God is a test of faith. But it is not an aspect of faith life that comes naturally. When we see a new dustup with God gathering on the horizon, our instinct is to run and hide. That is what Adam and Eve did when they felt the first pangs of a guilty conscience. They were afraid they would be crushed in an encounter with their Creator. And He could have done just that. God knew what they had done. Instead, He came into the garden offering hope for the arrival of a Champion—the Messiah whom He would send to save them from their own disobedience.

If wrestling with God is a test of our faith, it is also a test of God's faithfulness. "Put Me to the test, says the LORD of hosts, [see] if I will not open the windows of heaven for you and pour down for you a blessing until there is no more need" (Malachi 3:10). He wants our pleas for mercy and our petitions for renewal. "If two of you agree on earth about anything they ask," says Jesus, "it will be done for them by My Father in heaven" (Matthew 18:19). The word *anything* promises the infinite bounty of God's good gifts—His entire warehouse of blessings.

The critical responsibility of the parental role is to teach children to understand that their wrestling matches with God are opportunities, and then to grow from them.

Still, we do not relish these wrestling matches with God. They can be painful and bloody, troubling and self-convicting, exhausting and debilitating. They expose our weakness, remind us of our sin, humble us, and disturb our peace. We need them still. If we are to grow, if our character is to become truly godly, our wrestling matches with God are indispensable.[12]

Our kids also need to embrace their periodic wrestling matches with God, just as you and I do. If we do their wrestling for them, we do our children a great disservice. The critical responsibility of the parental role is to teach children to understand that their wrestling matches with God are opportunities, and then to grow from them. They, too, need the blessing of having a personal relationship with the Stranger who always wins. They need that relationship to be as intimate

12 In James 4:6–10: "But He gives more grace. Therefore it says, 'God opposes the proud but gives grace to the humble.' Submit yourselves therefore to God. Resist the devil, and he will flee from you. Draw near to God, and He will draw near to you. Cleanse your hands, you sinners, and purify your hearts, you double-minded. Be wretched and mourn and weep. Let your laughter be turned to mourning and your joy to gloom. Humble yourselves before the Lord, and He will exalt you."

as any wrestling match. For only then, when the Stranger wins, will they never lose.

Paul understood why this had to happen in his own life:

> We rejoice in hope of the glory of God. Not only that, but we rejoice in our sufferings, knowing that suffering produces endurance, and endurance produces character, and character produces hope, and hope does not put us to shame, because God's love has been poured into our hearts through the Holy Spirit who has been given to us. For while we were still weak, at the right time Christ died for the ungodly. For one will scarcely die for a righteous person—though perhaps for a good person one would dare even to die—but God shows His love for us in that while we were still sinners, Christ died for us. (Romans 5:2–8)

As the sun began to break over the horizon, the Stranger touched Jacob's hip. He could have killed Jacob with a word, so this touch was not intended as a deathblow. But it was painful. The limp in Jacob's stride would, no doubt, remind him of this night for the rest of his life. And still Jacob persisted. "I will not let You go unless You bless me."

> "What is your name?" asked the Stranger.
>
> "Heel-grabber," answered Jacob.
>
> Then the Stranger blessed him. "Your name shall no longer be called Jacob, but Israel, for you have striven with God and with men, and have prevailed."

If you're like me, you are probably saying to yourself, "That's it? A new name is all Jacob received for his effort?" It certainly doesn't sound like much of a reward for going toe-to-toe with the Almighty all night. How about a rhinestone-studded, golden-buckled belt with the inscription WORLD CHAMPION or a glass of cold milk and a kiss on the cheek from a pretty girl? On first blush, and given the hostile circumstances of a wrestling match to the death, God's changing of Jacob's name to Israel seems rather insignificant—a throwaway factoid to the main event. The new name even sounds a little contrived, until one looks closer at the blessing God is giving Jacob—a blessing that neither Jacob or you or I or any of God's people living in the twenty-first century fully understands in all of its glorious implications. But names matter. It's worth our time and effort to try to understand what those implications are. The name with which God blessed Jacob was one of the most significant names of all time.

ISRAEL'S CHILD

The new name God gave to Jacob stuck as a family marker for the entire Hebrew nation. Jacob's descendants came to be known as the "children of Israel." These were the people who wrestled with God daily for the simple necessities of life: food, water, shelter, protection, and spiritual sustenance.

Still not impressed? Try this. While most of us do not have Hebrew blood flowing through our veins, we are spiritually tied to Jacob's family as God's chosen people. By virtue of our faith, and not by ancestry, we rightfully bear the name Israel: "Ones Who Wrestle with God." When you and I study our Bibles, God is coming into our lives for an intimate wrestling match. When we call on His name in prayer, we are Gentiles who can legitimately claim the name "children of Israel" because we have been grafted in.[13] God's people are persistent in humbly begging for His blessings. As a matter of fact, our periodic wrestling matches with God are a privilege that only believers can experience. He comes into our lives, seeking to engage us, promising to bless us, testing us, touching us with the good news of His saving grace, shaping our character, and preparing us for what lies ahead.

When you and I study our Bibles, God is coming into our lives for an intimate wrestling match.

If you are still underwhelmed by the importance of this narrative, perhaps you will be impressed with this. At the beginning of Luke's Gospel, there are no less than four references to the name Israel or Jacob, all crammed onto perhaps a single page of Scripture. All four citations are tethered to Jesus' birth.[14] That is, they connect the nativity of Christ to the Old Testament blessing and Jacob's new name. The reason is the newborn infant, whom we annually worship as He humbly lies there in a food box for animals, in the little town of Bethlehem. That child, named Jesus, springs directly from Jacob's ancestral line. God had said He would use Abraham's family tree to send a Deliverer into our sin-rotted world. The Christ Child carried Israel's name as a Jew. In fact, not only was He one of the many Hebrews labeled "Ones Who Wrestle with God," but He was also *the* Offspring God had promised, the Deliverer from sin, death, and Satan's power, the One who would willingly wrestle with God to the death on our behalf.

Are you carrying a heavy burden in life? Jesus says come to Him. Let Him wrestle alongside of you and for you. Are you overwhelmed by temptation? In a fight with evil, you should know you cannot win. He has stood and will stand up

13 See Romans 11:17–24.

14 See Luke 1:33, 54–55, 68; 2:30–32.

to the powers of darkness for you and with you. Have you given up hope because the world has gone berserk in unbelief? Take heart; He has overcome the world. Do you have doubts about your faith? Receive the gifts of the Spirit and let your confidence in His promises soar.

When we wrestle with the Stranger, God always wins; yet, you can never lose. In His victory, you will continue to receive His blessings—even when it hurts.[15]

15 For a brief Bible study that examines the Christian's "victory lap," consider 1 John 5:4–5; 1 Corinthians 15:53–56; Psalm 60:12; Romans 8:35–38; John 16:33; Revelation 17:14.

For no one can lay a foundation other than that which is laid, which is Jesus Christ.

—1 Corinthians 3:11

CHAPTER 6

Built on the Rock

"Whoever tells the stories, defines the culture."[1] Depending on the storyteller, this can be good news or bad. So, whose story is shaping your life and your family's faith culture? Jesus used a parable to help us begin to explore this question:

> Everyone then who hears these words of Mine and does them will be like a wise man who built his house on the rock. And the rain fell, and the floods came, and the winds blew and beat on that house, but it did not fall, because it had been founded on the rock. And everyone who hears these words of Mine and does not do them will be like a foolish man who built his house on the sand. And the rain fell, and the floods came, and the winds blew and beat against that house, and it fell, and great was the fall of it. (Matthew 7:24–27)

There are two kinds of builders in Jesus' parable: wise and foolish. The wise builder constructs his spiritual house on the solid foundation of Jesus, the most profoundly honest storyteller in world history. In contrast, the foolish builder constructs his house to meet his short-term needs. He doesn't even pay attention to the kind of foundation he has chosen to build on.

Similarly, there are only two foundations: solid rock and sandy soil. Solid rock is Bible truth—God's truth. Airtight. Changeless. Eternal. Absolute. The sandy

1 David Walsh et al., *Dr. Dave's Cyberhood: Making Media Choices That Create a Healthy Electronic Environment for Your Kids* (New York: Simon and Schuster, 2001), 43.

soil of human truth has a relatively brief shelf life. Human truth is a slippery slope that leads to doubt, disappointment, and spiritual death.

God's template for the human creature included some freedoms. The freedom to make moral choices is a privilege and an honor. Many of our choices in life have nothing to do with good and evil. Human wisdom is up to the task of providing good advice for such decisions. But there are also many ethical choices that will need to be made on any given day. In the eyes of God, there are only two moral possibilities—right or wrong—for every ethical decision. Never both. Never neither.

Human truth is a slippery slope that leads to doubt, disappointment, and spiritual death.

Moral rightness is God's department. His standards are sky high; He demands flawless perfection.

There isn't much guessing about this parable's meaning. Jesus wants to be our Storyteller. His holy narrative—all of it—serves as the moral foundation for the lives of His people.[2]

But does the same principle that Jesus applied to these two homebuilders also apply to choosing a foundation for a house that would accommodate the builders' families? Introducing spouses, children, and maybe a few grandparents or aunts and uncles changes the conversation from the character of the individual builders to a discussion about family cultures. Wouldn't we all agree that's a whole new ballgame? Every individual living in either household has a unique worldview. Each family member sees his or her life from a slightly different angle. In fact, as is the case with most family cultures, one could safely bet they will never agree on everything. And some of them may not be able to agree on anything.

To wrestle with this question, we will go back to Scripture to examine two unique communities. And before we get started, we will admit from the outset that neither of the cultures we are about to study responded to either God's promises or His blessings in a way that anyone would describe as God pleasing. Yet, one of them can legitimately be called a godly culture. The other clearly is not. The assignment is to determine what distinguishes a godly culture from an ungodly culture. Our perspective is through the eyes and ears of the Bible, meaning we will try to base our judgment on the way God sees things.

2 Read Matthew 28:20. Consider the emphasis on the words "teaching them to observe all that I have commanded you."

CASE NO. 1: BABEL

After coming down from Mount Ararat, where the ark had come to rest, Noah and his family traveled east, settling on a fertile plain between the headwaters of the Tigris and Euphrates Rivers. The area in which they settled has been known in antiquity as Mesopotamia. On a modern map of the Middle East, Noah's clan settled in either eastern Syria or northern Iraq.

God blessed Noah's offspring, echoing the first time He blessed His human creatures in Eden. God had said they should spread abroad and repopulate the new earth.[3] But the generations that followed Noah and his family remained together in one community, ignoring God's will. Soon the storytellers of this community were diminishing God's role as humankind's deliverer from the flood. They began, instead, to emphasize the remarkable achievements of human technology to build an ark of such dimensions—one that could withstand such a destructive deluge. The storytellers wanted to promote the idea that the future of their community rested in humankind's ingenuity. Apparently, their intent was to build a monument to honor human progress. A massive tower seemed like a good idea because it would offer a kind of mountaintop view from a terrain that seemed endlessly flat. Here is how Moses chronicled the event for posterity:

> Now the whole earth had one language and the same words. And as people migrated from the east, they found a plain in the land of Shinar and settled there. And they said to one another, "Come, let us make bricks, and burn them thoroughly." And they had brick for stone, and bitumen for mortar. Then they said, "Come, let us build ourselves a city and a tower with its top in the heavens, and let us make a name for ourselves, lest we be dispersed over the face of the whole earth." And the LORD came down to see the city and the tower, which the children of man had built. And the LORD said, "Behold, they are one people, and they have all one language, and this is only the beginning of what they will do. And nothing that they propose to do will now be impossible for them. Come, let Us go down and there confuse their language, so that they may not understand one another's speech." So the LORD dispersed them from there over the face of all the earth, and they left off building the city. Therefore its name was called Babel, because there the LORD

3 Given the circumstances and thrust of Genesis 9:7, God's words are laced with the force of law. To ignore His will that the population should disperse must be understood as an act of willful disobedience.

> confused the language of all the earth. And from there the LORD dispersed them over the face of all the earth. (Genesis 11:1–9)

The storytellers in Babel understood that it was their unity that held their community together. Unity was one of their core values. Their common language was a critical factor in maintaining their sense of unity. Their rationale had a convincing objective: "Come . . . let us make a name for ourselves, lest we be dispersed over the face of the whole earth."

Babel's storytellers gave people a reason to feel good about the future by giving them a plan for galvanizing their community around a common goal. Meanwhile, the God of Noah's deliverance had been quietly eliminated from their community's narrative. Moreover, His command to Noah's offspring to repopulate the earth had, for all practical purposes, been overturned with a new plan. In other words, their community had become a godless, secular culture.

Technology also played an important role in this event. This is important because the culture we live in knows a thing or two about technology's impact. Here we will want to be careful about how we discuss the role technology plays in the development of any culture. For one thing, human imagination is a gift from God. The ability to think, analyze, deliberate, design, and implement was a blessing tailor made to assist mankind in overseeing God's creation. Furthermore, in its original state, human imagination was just as perfect as the rest of creation. Only after the human race became enslaved in sin did humans begin to use their imagination to discredit God's narrative.

Only after the human race became enslaved in sin did humans begin to use their imagination to discredit God's narrative.

In Babel, the human inventions of kiln-fired brick and tar-pitch mortar combined to create an opportunity for doing something truly remarkable. Given the technological advances, the concept was certainly doable. The historical record seems also to suggest that the invention of cuneiform writing greatly enhanced the ability of designers and builders to communicate with one another accurately, making the technical aspect of the project quite doable. With the necessary technology in place, the call for unity gave the project a clear rationale. All in all, this was a superb marketing campaign and a shameless promotion of communal advancement. When completed, people would be able to climb to the top of this celebrated structure to view the entire valley. The achievement would be seen as a noble project—hailed, perhaps, as a giant leap forward for humankind.

Though God knew exactly what was happening in their unbelieving hearts, the biblical report refuses to indict Babel's storytellers for immoral practices. Yet, we get a strong indication of God's deep concern regarding their godless behavior when we are, once again, invited to listen in on one of those brief meetings of the Holy Trinity, where the discussion considers how to deal with Babel's secular storytellers. "Behold, they are one people, and they have all one language, and this is only the beginning of what they will do. And nothing that they propose to do will now be impossible for them. Come, let Us go down and there confuse their language, so that they may not understand one another's speech" (Genesis 11:6–7).

If sinful people are permitted to advance their own story without restraint and take the credit for their progress, their imagination will inevitably lead them to do godless things and believe godless teachings.

God knows His human creatures well. If sinful people are permitted to advance their own story without restraint and take the credit for their progress, their imagination will inevitably lead them to do godless things and believe godless teachings. The time will come when the human race will finally destroy itself through mankind's own foolish self-glorification. God simply could not allow that to happen. His plan to save sinners would have been in jeopardy. So, He lovingly intervened. And His intervention bears witness to His own commitment to keep the promise He had made to Adam and Eve. It is important to remember that this was a promise God had also made to Himself.[4] His divine reputation was at stake.

The confounding of Babel's language flowed from God's heart of love and demonstrates His profound patience with His sinful creatures. The unintelligible languages the Babelonians were suddenly speaking were in their best long-term interest. God's interventions are usually aimed at averting an impending disaster. Yet, God's confounding of their languages is often construed as an act of divine punishment. And, truly, it is that. God's hates the sin of unbelief more than any other sin.[5] But the big story here is a story of God's love in the face of sin, for this divine Judge was sparing the lives of Babel's population to give them more time to repent for their sin of unbelief and flee to His mercy. In this respect, then, the narrative is an explanation of divine grace and a demonstration of God's holy patience.

God's response to Babel's tower plan was also in keeping with His will that the human race should multiply and spread abroad on the earth. As we have already established, His will is always done. Confusing their ability to communicate with

4 See Hebrews 6:17–20.

5 For a brief Bible study on the sin of unbelief, consider the following texts: Deuteronomy 32:20; Hosea 8:12–13; John 3:36; 8:24; Hebrews 3:12; 1 John 2:22–23.

one another had the effect of dispersing Babel's population to the far ends of the earth. If Babel's plan was to stubbornly ignore God's will, He would use a more forceful way to get them to conform to His will.

By confusing their ability to communicate, their jealous God checked an entire society that was hell-bent on inventing a new narrative that touted human ingenuity and imagination as a replacement for God's story of unbounded love and unending blessing.[6] When unbelievers write the story, it is destined to be a narrative of self-deception, self-glorification, and self-worship. When God writes the story, His grace is always at the heart of the narrative.

When God writes the story, His grace is always at the heart of the narrative.

Our age is a cauldron of new paradigms. Some people say we are living in a rewind of the Babel narrative. Yes, it is true that humankind has made some notable progress. Human imagination deserves some of the credit. The advancements in physics, medicine, genetic engineering, space and aeronautics, digital communication, and other technologies cannot be ignored. Of course, such advancements are the result of the abilities God has given us, which make it possible for us to innovate. He has a legitimate right to all the glory for what He has done. If history is rehearsed with integrity, the record will also show that, in spite of human progress, humankind has failed to deal with the most significant issues of life on our planet.[7] Apart from God, spiritual peace remains elusive. Injustice persists. Crime runs rampant. Greed is epidemic. The human race is still mired in its struggle to find an answer to death. Yet, we murder one another and sometimes ourselves. Without Christ, there is no escaping the long-term effects of human immorality. This is not a pessimistic spin on our status; it is an honest evaluation. It can foolishly be debunked or dismissed, but it cannot be dismissed for being untrue. The tragedy is compounded when the seeds of a false and godless hope are sown and people are deceived into believing that such achievements are still within our human grasp. This is the false gospel that humanism continues to spread in our secular age. Jesus called it "building on sandy soil." And He accurately labeled the storytellers of such fables simpletons and fools.

---

6 For a brief Bible study about divine jealousy, consider Exodus 20:5; 34:14; Deuteronomy 4:24; 6:15; Joshua 24:19; Ezekiel 23:25; 2 Corinthians 11:2.

7 One lesson that must be relearned by each succeeding generation is the lesson of two historical perspectives. In one perspective, humankind chronicles history as a narrative that is completely homocentric. The second historical perspective focuses on progress that is exclusively rooted in God's loving faithfulness to intervene in human affairs.

CASE NO. 2: ISRAEL IN THE SINAI WILDERNESS

Our second case study covers a narrow sliver of world history that lasted only forty years. The biblical narrative of this period is often referred to as "the exodus."

The narrative recounts the wanderings of the children of Israel in the Sinai wilderness. In this setting, God was the only hope for perhaps as many as three million men, women, and children. The accounts are written in Moses' hand. In his telling, there is no doubt that this is God's story.[8]

After spending four hundred years as a satellite of the pagan Egyptian Empire, the Hebrews needed to see their faithful God's redemptive power. They needed Him to intervene on their behalf. For the next forty years, they received massive doses of what they needed most: I AM's loving embrace.

This is the only time in human history when God directed the culture of an entire society. It is called a *theocracy*, which means "governed by God." During this era, and only among the children of Israel, God's narrative was the only story in town. And the approach God took for shaping Israel's culture and conveying His message of loving faithfulness used a combined media that engaged all five senses. By that, we mean that the children of Israel were literally able to see, hear, feel, taste, and smell God's living presence among them every single day. In fact, it would have been impossible for them to miss Him. Their entire culture was saturated with a narrative that echoed I AM's presence. He formed their worship life, framing it with fragrant incense and aromatic oils to anoint His chosen leaders. He prescribed their moral code, established their civil and religious laws, provided a nutritious diet, structured their educational model, rendered the dimensions for the tabernacle's architecture and furnishings, gave the people meaningful rituals, ordained their religious feasts, inaugurated the priesthood, maintained camp security, oversaw the Israelites' political structure, and guided their progress.

God's plan to deliver His Hebrew people from Pharaoh's stubborn grip was hardly subtle. He instructed Moses to tell Pharaoh to let the Hebrews leave Egypt so they could worship Him in the desert. When Pharaoh refused, God sent the first of ten plagues (Exodus 7–12), turning the mighty Nile into a river of blood. And it wasn't just the Nile River that ran dead red. Egypt's entire water system turned to blood, including the water at the bottom of wooden buckets and ceram-

8 Like the Babel narrative, the Hebrew culture during this period is fairly easy to analyze because it is so thoroughly isolated by geography and circumstance. But the reader needs to be careful about making too much of such isolation. Israel's isolation was part of God's training rigor. I AM was preparing them for their new life in their own homeland. Such isolation is not a signal for God's people to flock to a monastery or cloister their families in remote lifestyles to protect their offspring from the unbelieving world. God wants His people rubbing elbows with our unbelieving neighbors. He wants us spreading His Gospel to those who still live in the darkness of unbelief.

ic jars. Fish died in the river for lack of oxygen. The stench of decaying blood and piles of rotting fish became unbearable.

When Pharaoh relented, only to change his mind, God sent a second calamity to devastate the land with frogs. The Bible says, "They gathered them together in heaps, and the land stank" (Exodus 8:14). Following the plague of frogs came massive swarms of gnats. This was followed by flies, dead livestock, painful boils, hail, clouds of locusts, and darkness so thick people could actually feel it. The ordeal went on and on; yet, Pharaoh kept hardening his heart until God finally caused Pharaoh's heart to harden, even before his time of grace on earth officially ended in his death.

God's tenth plague sent a powerful message that would have long-term implications for the entire human race. In this last plague, God's angel of death took the life of the firstborn male of every Egyptian family, including Pharaoh's firstborn son. Where Hebrew families had smeared a slaughtered lamb's blood on the wooden crossbeams that framed the doors of their slave quarters, the firstborn males were spared. The imagery of blood-stained wood projected forward to Christ, God's sacrificial Lamb, whose blood drained onto the timbers of a crude Roman cross.

Over the next four decades, God's daily presence among His people would be unmistakable. When Pharaoh's army threatened to overrun the Hebrews, God sent a wind to open a path—an escape route of dry land through the middle of the Red Sea. The Israelites lived to see another day; Pharaoh's army drowned (Exodus 14:13–31).

In the desert, God fed His people daily with quail and sweet manna (Exodus 16). He provided drinking water from a rock (Exodus 17). When God punished the people for their constant grumbling by sending venomous snakes among them, He also graciously offered a remedy from the deadly snakebites, telling Moses to make a bronze pole with a carved snake on it. When those who had been bitten looked at the bronze pole, they lived. New Testament believers in Jesus eventually saw that this bronze pole was a picture of God's promise to send a Savior, who would be lifted up on a cross to provide healing and hope to all who believed His words.[9]

At Mount Sinai, where God gave His Ten Commandments to the people, the mountaintop was covered in thick, black clouds of smoke, and the people heard the sound of trumpets. Thunder boomed, lightning flashed, and the earth shook all around the perimeter of the mountain. I AM issued a warning that the people should not follow Moses up the mountainside, lest they be consumed by His holi-

9 See John 3:14–15 and 8:27–30.

ness. He instructed Moses to have a fence constructed around the mountain's perimeter to restrain those who thought about ignoring God's warning (Exodus 19).

For their worship life, God ordered a portable tent called the tabernacle. It was to be placed at the center of the camp for all to see. Inside the tabernacle, the holiest place held a large wooden box called the ark of the covenant. The ark was covered in gold, and on the top was the Mercy Seat, depicting two supernatural creatures called cherubim—another visual symbol of God's promise to send a Savior (Exodus 25–26).

Each day, sacrifices were made by the priests at sunrise and sunset (Exodus 29:39). And each evening, Aaron and his sons recited a trinitarian *shalom*: "The LORD bless you and keep you; the LORD make His face to shine upon you and be gracious to you; the LORD lift up His countenance upon you and give you peace" (Numbers 6:22–27). Aaron's nightly benediction echoed God's first blessing to Adam and Eve. It reminded the Israelites that I AM was still committed to blessing them daily with His good gifts.

God was a 24/7 presence. For forty years, God's people were constantly exposed to the simple truth that God loved them, even though they did not deserve His love. That truth was practiced in their daily routine, reinforced in their annual celebrations, and emphasized in their prayer life.

One would think the children of Israel would have learned the lesson. Yet, time and again, they turned away from God, grumbling about their meager desert existence, fomenting reasons to disobey and rebel.

By analysis, both cultures seem flawed. At times, the children of Israel behaved as though they were a godless nation. While Moses was up on Mount Sinai receiving instructions from God, the Israelites below were bowing down to a golden calf that Aaron had fashioned from gold plundered from their Egyptian masters. That golden calf resembled the likeness of one of the Egyptians' most popular false gods (Exodus 32). Are we left then to conclude that God's experiment in theocratic culture-building was a resounding failure?

Hardly. Many of the people who lived through the forty-year trek grew in their faith in God's promises. God's will was done then, just as it is done in our day. His story was and is today remembered. His faithfulness was then, and is in our lifetime, chronicled for future generations to rehearse and recite. We are still reading the exodus narrative today, learning the lessons God wants us to learn from His people's ancient experiences. And, as we share these stories with our own children and grandchildren, we grow in our understanding of God's love for us. And our faith in His sure promises is strengthened. We are living proof that God's masterful plan for making sure that future generations would never forget what He has done for His people has been a success.

We are living proof that God's masterful plan for making sure that future generations would never forget what He has done for His people has been a success.

In Deuteronomy 4:9, we hear God establishing a theme that would stand as a universal principle for all time. "Take care, and keep your soul diligently, lest you forget the things that your eyes have seen, and lest they depart from your heart all the days of your life. Make them known to your children and your children's children."[10] The people who lived through the wilderness ordeal took some profound spiritual images with them, along with the sounds and smells and tastes of God's gracious presence. These metaphors were seared into their memories.

You and I are likewise encouraged to share the life experiences of God's grace working its miracle to transform our hearts and restore our lives with His forgiveness and love.

So how shall we distinguish Israel's forty-year narrative in the Sinai from the Babel story? Which culture was the godly culture? Maybe the more important question is what made one culture godly and the other culture ungodly?

One of these two cultures made a conscious decision to replace the divine Storyteller with stories and storytellers of human origin. The Babel narrative was fraudulent. Israel, on the other hand, was permeated for four decades with a narrative that was timeless and alive with the wonder of I AM's unearned and undeserved love. While His people proved to be unfaithful, I AM, the divine Storyteller, was always true to His Word.

GOD'S NEW TESTAMENT CULTURE

The Babel narrative closed with a big, fat thud. The community with the grandiose idea of branding itself as the home of the first great wonder of the post-deluge world was dispersed. But the Bible is also honest in reporting the terrible idolatry that later ran rampant among God's people, when Israel's kings adopted the godless practices of their pagan neighbors. The Jews, once a proud and powerful nation of God's people, were dragged off into captivity. Only a remnant returned to Jerusalem seventy years later, to a humbler version of Jewish culture.

10 Known as "the Great Shema" or "Shema Yisrael," Deuteronomy 6:4 echoes the command "Hear, O Israel!" A message similar to Deuteronomy 6:4–9 is repeated in Deuteronomy 11:13–21 and Numbers 15:37–41 and Malachi 4:4–6. Practicing Jews consider the Shema to be the most important part of their worship life and their final thought before going to sleep. Christians understand these words as an overarching principle regarding the family's firm commitment to remain rooted in God's Word. The main thought of the Shema is that we must pass on the truths of what God has done for us to the next generation. The Christian Church Year is an example of how Christians integrate the commemorative narrative of God's work into our annual worship life.

In the short view, it is hard to understand what, if anything, the wandering Israelite population of the exodus has to do with us. But from a biblical perspective, something very precious has survived the Israelites' desert experience—something we still celebrate today. While God's presence is no longer visible in the radiant columns of smoke and fire, the bright light of God's holy presence occurs daily among His people, smack in the middle of a dark and forbidding world of unbelief that behaves like the Antichrist. That brilliant light lives on today in the community we know as the Christian Church on earth.[11]

The Christian Church is a divinely ordained institution. It was planned in eternity by the consensus of our triune God. At once, the Church is a community, a society, a family of believers, and a culture.[12] God's Church is found wherever His Word is faithfully taught and the Sacraments are diligently practiced.[13] The visible Church—God's created kingdom on earth—is a tangible entity, observable in the divine message it proclaims. Because of its spiritual nature, we can understand that God's kingdom lives in the hearts of sinners like us, who have been remade as God's children through the power of faith in His sure promises.

Like Israel, the Christian Church is far from perfect. But its people know and believe that they have been washed clean in Jesus' blood. This conviction is what binds us to Him. It is also what binds us together as God's people.[14]

The urgent call for a serious family conversation includes a tough-love discussion about our own godless performance that contradicts our identity as God's children.

In the Church's embrace, applying Bible truth to daily life describes the Spirit's ongoing work of forming godly character in God's people.[15] The culture of today's world

11 God's Church is sometimes distinguished in two unique dimensions. The first is as the Church Militant, where the battle for human souls is fought daily by God's people through the ministry of Word and the Sacraments. The future Church that exists in God's eternal, spiritual realm is referred to as the Church Triumphant. In the Church Triumphant, time, space, and change cease to exist; the daily battle to preserve souls also ends because sin no longer taints human thought and behavior. In the Church Triumphant, the Lamb's victory celebration continues forever in heaven's glory.

12 Lange, *God So Loved*, 643. Lange writes, "The gospel is the tool God uses to change hearts, give salvation, and preserve faith. It is the means by which the church is to carry out its mission (Ro 1:16). The church also preaches the law of God, but this is done in the interest of preparing the way for the preaching of the gospel."

13 Lange, *God So Loved*, 535.

14 See Matthew 16:16–18 and Romans 15:5–7.

15 Though similar, character formation and sanctification are not synonymous. Believers and unbelievers both undergo a character formation process. The theological term associated with the Holy Spirit's work of calling, converting, cleansing, gathering, and enlightening human hearts is called *sanctification*. Only believers experience the radical change of heart that transforms them, by the power of God's truth, into His (spiritually) chosen people.

mitigates against this biblical understanding of the relationships God's people have with one another.[16] Sadly, there are too many examples of how God's people treat one another in a loveless manner. Our behaviors too often highlight the divisions, schisms, and disagreements. We choose, too frequently, to wrestle with one another instead of wrestling with God to find ways to resolve our differences. Like the children of Israel, God's Church on earth often betrays our Lord Jesus with loveless family feuds. The urgent call for a serious family conversation includes a tough-love discussion about our own godless performance that contradicts our identity as God's children.

16 For a brief Bible study on the topic of Christian unity, consider these texts: 1 Corinthians 1:10; 10:17; Ephesians 4:3, 13; Romans 12:5; Galatians 3:28; Philippians 1:27; 1 Peter 3:8.

I warn everyone who hears the words of the prophecy of this book: if anyone adds to them, God will add to him the plagues described in this book, and if anyone takes away from the words of the book of this prophecy, God will take away his share in the tree of life and in the holy city, which are described in this book.

—Revelation 22:18–19

CHAPTER 7

Yeast Beast

In Eden, the character of our first ancestors was flawless. The balance and order of their character matched perfectly the **C = I + P** formula for character (character equals identity plus performance). They radiated their Creator's holy image with hearts beating pure and in perfect rhythm to His righteous will.[1] Love, the very essence of their Creator God, made Adam and Eve who they were. Love drove their every thought, conversation, and activity. Their Maker was pleased.

The immoral choice Adam and Eve made ruined everything. The beautiful relationship they enjoyed with God was gone. Guilt washed over them like a tidal wave. They were ashamed, and their consciences refused to excuse them. They trembled in fear, with good reason. God had said that if they disobeyed His command not to eat from the tree of the knowledge of good and evil, they would surely die.

Sin is serious business. There is no point in continuing our conversation if we cannot acknowledge sin's impact. It would be foolish to dismiss either sin or sin's most horrible consequences as though they were merely speed bumps on the road of life. Sin is real.

---

1 John C. Jeske, *Genesis*, The People's Bible (Milwaukee: Northwestern Publishing House, 2001), 24–25. For sinful people, it is difficult to understand what is all entailed in bearing "the image of God." Jeske writes, "Unlike the mental dullness and ignorance we bring with us into the world, Adam and Eve understood perfectly with their *intellect* what God wanted them to know. While they possessed the image of God, their *emotions* were also in tune with God's; they found their greatest happiness in God. And, unlike the rebellious will each of us brought into the world, their *will* was in complete harmony with God; what he wanted was what they wanted. Every impulse and desire of theirs was in tune with God's good will. Created in the image of God, they were human replicas of what God is like."

After the fall, human hearts were so thoroughly corrupted by sin that people sought ways to turn God's template for character upside down.[2] In God's formula, identity always rises above performance. Answering the question "Who am I?" is a prerequisite and paramount to answering the question "What should I do?" Sinful mankind was bent on overturning that ordered process. After the fall, doing became very important. Identity became an afterthought.[3] Our ancestors now had to learn how to hunt for food, defend themselves from some animals and domesticate others. They harvested fruits, vegetables, and roots. Shelters had to be built, clothing made, babies tended. Performance. Performance. Performance. People began to rely so much on their own cunning performances that some of them stopped trusting God to bless them.

In God's formula, identity always rises above performance.

Folks soon discovered that anything done well left favorable impressions on others. They began to polish their own public images to impress their neighbors. In the twisted human understanding of character, a good impression seemed like the equivalent to good character. Even those who believed God's promise saw the value of having a fine public reputation. People began to refine their people skills and put in the extra hours just to do things that would impress others. The Bible does not tell us this is wrong. In fact, there are many passages in Scripture that encourage us to nurture traits that will leave a fine, lasting impression. It can be a way to glorify God. Scripture does, however, warn us not to replace God by setting ourselves up as idols.

The reversal from **C = I + P** to **C = P + I** was so subtle that it probably happened without notice[4]. Nevertheless, the shift in how people understood good character took a heavy hit, as performance dominated identity, and the importance of knowing one's personal identity diminished. People knew what they could do without knowing who they were. But, here's the worst part: the new, distorted version of God's original template for human character fostered the false notion that sinful human beings could somehow behave their way back into

2 Jeske, *Genesis*, 46. Jeske writes, "God had been unbelievably generous to Adam and Eve, but there was one thing he had not given them—equality with himself. They were not God. God had designed them to live under him, not alongside him."

3 In Genesis 4:21–22, we learn that people were being remembered for what they did for a living: Jubal was a musician, and Tubal-cain forged all instruments of bronze and iron.

4 Students in algebra classes are taught that in the order of two or more addends does not change the result. In other words, 3 + 4 and 4 + 3 both equal 7. In God's worldview, the order of Identity and Performance matters greatly. Mankind is not at liberty to change the Creator's ordained order. See Isaiah 55:8.

God's favor. Ever since, Satan has whispered this perverse lie into every human ear: *If you perform well, you can placate God with your good deeds and regain His goodwill.* Of course, nothing could be more untrue. God demands perfection. No sinful human being is capable of achieving it. Into this world of distorted truth and sinful depravity, I AM sent His Son. It is time to meet Him.

WHERE'S THE BREAD?

Jesus had just fed more than four thousand hungry people with seven loaves of bread and a few small fish. This was the second time in just a few weeks that He had done such a remarkable thing. Now, crowds followed Him everywhere. The people wanted to make Him their bread king.

One morning, a group of Jewish leaders came looking for Jesus. Matthew notes it was a mixed group of Pharisees and Sadducees. This is important because it was unusual to see members of these two Jewish sects together. They had an intense dislike for each other. But their willingness to join forces on this day shows they hated Jesus more than they hated each other. Their plan was to entrap Him. As bait, they asked Him to give them a sign from heaven—something astounding and unexplainable—another miracle to prove once and for all that He was the Son of God.[5] Jesus responded by noting that they could forecast the weather quite well but were unable to understand His prophetic reference to the prophet Jonah as a picture of the resurrection (Matthew 16:2–4). Then He walked away, leaving the religious leaders to chew on the phrase "the sign of Jonah." They knew exactly what Jesus was referring to and why.[6]

Later the same day, we find Jesus and His disciples crossing the Sea of Galilee. Halfway across, they discovered that someone had forgotten to bring the bread for lunch. Amid the disciples' groaning and complaining, Jesus could be heard saying something that sounded important: "Watch and beware of the leaven of the Pharisees and Sadducees" (Matthew 16:6). He was obviously still reflecting on His conversation with the Jewish leaders earlier that day. Some of His disciples thought He was warning them not to buy the yeasty bread sold in the outer courts of the temple.[7] Seeing their confusion, Jesus explained that, if they thought His

---

5 These religious leaders were using a tactic similar to the devil's tactic to tempt Jesus in the wilderness. They were allies of the devil—the serpent's offspring that God referred to when he declared his enmity with Satan in Genesis 3:15.

6 This is the second time a mixed group of Jewish leaders challenged Jesus to give them a sign to prove He was the Messiah. In Matthew 12:18–45, Jesus explains that the sign of Jonah is a symbolic reference to His three-day burial in the belly of the earth before His resurrection (12:40). The Sadducees, in particular, had a problem with what Jesus was saying because they did not believe in life beyond the grave. Their worldview did not accept transcendency.

7 It was common knowledge that the temple leaders improved their profit margin by adding extra yeast to puff up each batch of dough.

remark was about forgotten bread, they needed to trust Him to provide for their needs. It was a gentle reminder of the miracles He had done just a few days earlier.

If the disciples had been listening, they would have known the Master's comment was not about bread at all. It was about yeast. He was using yeast, and its effect on bread, to picture a dangerous practice. Something in the Pharisees' and Sadducees' interpretation of Scripture was jeopardizing their eternal future. Whatever it was, these religious leaders were infecting God's people with a deadly leaven of toxic teachings.

Every Jew knew that yeast was to be scorned and avoided one time every year. Fifteen centuries earlier, the first Passover had established the Passover tradition. Moses recorded God's instructions to the enslaved Hebrews in preparation for their exodus from Egypt. God said:

> This day shall be for you a memorial day, and you shall keep it as a feast to the Lord; throughout your generations, as a statute forever, you shall keep it as a feast. Seven days you shall eat unleavened bread. On the first day you shall remove leaven out of your houses, for if anyone eats what is leavened, from the first day until the seventh day, that person shall be cut off from Israel. On the first day you shall hold a holy assembly, and on the seventh day a holy assembly. No work shall be done on those days. But what everyone needs to eat, that alone may be prepared by you. And you shall observe the Feast of Unleavened Bread, for on this very day I brought your hosts out of the land of Egypt. . . . You shall eat nothing leavened; in all your dwelling places you shall eat unleavened bread. (Exodus 12:14–20)

Did you catch the passion and intensity of God's instructions? If a Hebrew family didn't comply, they were to be thrown out of the community. Why? What harm could a few stray morsels of yeasted bread crumbs do? And what is the big deal with eating leavened bread?[8]

The answer has to do with the godless environment God's people had been living in for the last four hundred years. With its cults, its pantheon of false gods, and its arrogant rulers who claimed godlike status, Egypt was hardly a good place for raising a godly family. Life in Egypt was a serious threat to the faith of God's people. They were living in a culture that was hostile to their faith. Some of them

---

8 Today, practicing Jews still observe the tradition of cleaning the house during the weeks before Passover. Unleavened bread is still a central part of the Seder meal. The yeastless bread signifies the cleansing of the sins—especially the sin of idolatry. The ritual symbolically shows their hearts are focused on God for their deliverance.

may have already brought the pagan pantheon into their own homes. The removal of yeast from their homes and diets was God's picture for teaching them that His deliverance from pagan Egypt had profound spiritual implications. He wanted them to know I AM as their emancipator from spiritual captivity. He wanted the godless Egyptian culture purged from their memory. He wanted them to serve as witnesses of the deliverance He was about to undertake on their behalf, so they could share that narrative with future generations.[9]

When Jesus made His remark about the yeast of the Pharisees and Sadducees, He was referring to the Passover. The religious ideas of these Jewish leaders were just as noxious to the faith of God's people living in Israel as the godless Egyptian rituals were to the Israelites living in Goshen. Jesus, the eternal Judge, was sitting in judgment of the spiritual character of both the Pharisees and Sadducees. He was warning His followers to beware of such false teachers and their godless teachings. Because their religion was based on a diabolical lie, these religious leaders were guilty of leading many of God's people into the jaws of hell.

We must not misunderstand Jesus' terse response as hateful or vengeful. He loved those Pharisees and Sadducees every bit as much as He loves us. And because He loved them, He was willing to speak the unvarnished truth to them. His purpose was to shake them to their core. He wanted them to repent of their sin of twisting His true Word. Their unbelieving and self-consuming attitudes were like yeast—ever growing, always spreading like the plague. They needed to change their worldview before their hearts would become so hard that they would no longer be open to God's saving truth.

The Sadducees

Lacking a worldview that included eternity and immortality, the foundation for any hope of living forever was an empty promise.

The Sadducees were rationalists. They worshiped human intellect. If they could not approach important life issues with logical analysis, the concept would be ignored. They denied large portions of the Old Testament Scriptures because many of these ancient teachings did not seem reasonable. Never mind that the Scriptures were understood as God's living Word! They still were worldviews rooted in transcendency and the promise of an enchanted, eternal Kingdom of grace. For these learned men, the Bible's teachings about life after death, and the resurrection, in particular, defied all logic. They rejected these biblical truths out of hand. Immor-

9 The entire nation of Israel would function as living witnesses to the wonders God performed over the forty years in the desert. Their eyewitness accounting of God's deliverance was similar to the eyewitness record of Jesus' life on earth by the apostles. (See Acts 1:1–9.)

tality and the promise of living with God forever seemed to be silly fantasies because they were inconsistent with human reason. As a result, the Sadducees' hope for a better future was limited to the time and space of earthly kingdoms. Lacking a worldview that included eternity and immortality, the foundation for any hope of living forever was an empty promise.

Christians live in the sure hope that God's promise for immortality transcends our temporary physical existence on earth. Eternal life has already been secured for us. Jesus told His dear friend Martha, "I am the resurrection and the life. Whoever believes in Me, though he die, yet shall he live" (John 11:25). With one exception, those who believe Jesus' promise are no better at forecasting future events than the rest of the earth's population. But the single exception is crucial. God's people know with absolute certainty that an eternal home is waiting for them in their future. The life-changing knowledge of our certain future with God in the new heavens and the new earth makes a major difference in how we see ourselves in the present world.

Christ's resurrection is necessary for understanding who we are. By dismissing the resurrection as fiction and limiting God's promises to the here and now of this temporary life on earth, the Sadducees denied the heart of a biblical truth.[10] And because they could not see their own eternal future, the Sadducees limited their faith life to doing good works. They settled for far less than God had promised with His gift of grace. Eternity was beyond the realm of their convictions. Leaving a good social impression on others was all they had left. The Sadducees used the concept of doing good works to reinforce communal standards and control everyday life in Jewish culture. Their utilitarian view of doing good was not unlike the approach taken by secular humanists in our American culture today.

The Pharisees

The Pharisees were also all about performance. They were legalists, forever harping on the details of the Mosaic Law and getting God's people to toe the line. They rested their hope in creating a better future by doing things that would impress both God and their neighbors.

The Pharisees believed in heaven and hell. But their way of getting to heaven was driven by human achievement. In fact, they were so sure that following God's "rulebook" would get them to heaven, they actually added new rules that seemed to have the force of God's Law.[11] Then they would proudly strut through the streets, appearing to be morally upright.

10 See 1 Corinthians 15:12–19.

11 Franzmann, *New Testament*, vol. 1, Bible History Commentary, 92–93. (See also Revelation 22:18–19.)

The Pharisees were classic examples of **C = P + I** thinking. According to their worldview, their identity depended, to a greater degree, on how good they were. They promoted the corrupt lie that people can restore themselves to God's eternal kingdom by virtue of their own good character.

The Pharisees were classic examples of C = P + I thinking.

The dream of shaping a better future for this life can be an honorable goal. Our world is filled with people who are suffering from the effects of disease and illness, catastrophic calamities, war, pestilence, injustice, poverty, tyranny. The work of helping others lends purpose and meaning to our earthly lives. It can give us joy and a sense of personal accomplishment. It is an expression of our selfless, Christlike love for all people. It serves as a positive example for our children to follow and provides opportunities to show compassion for people who need a helping hand. Jesus Himself told a parable about a Samaritan who went out of his way to help a stranger in need. But if we believe Satan's lie that doing good things for friends, neighbors, and strangers unlocks heaven's door, we are on a path that fails to see that Christ's life, death, and resurrection are the only way to secure immortality. If the ultimate goal is our resurrection from the dead and the life of the world to come (and it should be just that), Jesus is the only way.

The Pharisees' particular strain of spiritual yeast runs rampant in our American culture. Satan works overtime trying to convince people that doing good is their ticket into God's heavenly kingdom. Christians are especially vulnerable. Because it appeals to the false notion that we are in charge of saving our own souls, this kind of thinking can easily creep into our faith life.

All of us want kids who are selfless, compassionate people. Yet, if we are not careful, the yeast of the Pharisees will find its way into our homes to infect the members of our families. Jesus' warning to His disciples was also intended as a warning for us to take to heart. The distance between helping our children develop a God-pleasing character and raising little Pharisees can appear to be a fine line. It isn't. To mistake works-righteousness for God's grace is to take a detour that dead-ends in spiritual arrogance and certain disaster.

Veggie Tales creator Phil Vischer struggled with this false and misleading worldview. In an interview, Vischer was blunt to admit that the Christian message he was trying to teach children in his popular cartoon series wasn't Christianity at all.

> I looked back at the previous 10 years and realized I had spent 10 years trying to convince kids to behave Christianly without actually teaching them Christianity. And that was a pretty serious convic-

> tion. You can say, "Hey kids, be more forgiving because the Bible says so," or "Hey kids, be more kind because the Bible says so!" But that isn't Christianity, it's morality. . . .
>
> And that was such a huge shift for me from the American Christian ideal. We're drinking a cocktail that's a mix of the Protestant work ethic, the American dream, and the gospel. And we've intertwined them so completely that we can't tell them apart anymore. Our gospel has become a gospel of following your dreams and being good so God will make all your dreams come true. It's the Oprah god.[12]

Vischer's struggle is repeated among millions of people who claim they are Christians, who think that eternity will belong to them by virtue of all the good they have done in their lives. In a culture that rewards performance, we are easily confused between belonging to God's family because of His grace and earning His love by living morally upright lives.

God's Law tells us that our sinful condition makes it impossible for us to do anything to repair or restore the relationship with God that was lost in Eden. It reminds us that we are the lost, the least, the last, and the little people for whom Jesus came to earth. The Law tells us we have no hope for a blessed eternal future without Jesus. The Gospel lifts us from our hopelessness and despair, offering us full and free forgiveness and complete reconciliation with God. It tells us that Christ Jesus has performed all things necessary for our salvation. Making this distinction between the purpose for God's Law and the Good News of salvation in Christ's work alone is critical to our eternal future. It is equally as critical to the eternal future of our children.[13]

---

12 Barrett Johnson, "How to Raise a Pagan Kid in a Christian Home," INFO for Families, November 13, 2013, accessed May 7, 2016, http://www.infoforfamilies.com/blog/2013/11/13/how-to-raise-a-pagan-kid-in-a-christian-home#.UuBHYP16i-w=.

13 C. F. W. Walther, *God's No and God's Yes: The Proper Distinction between Law and Gospel* (St. Louis: Concordia Publishing House, 1973), 25. Walther says, "The moment we learn to know the distinction between the Law and the Gospel, it is as if the sun were rising upon the Scriptures, and we behold all the contents of the Scriptures in the most beautiful harmony. We see that the Law was not revealed to us to put the notion into our heads that we can become righteous by it, but to teach us that we are utterly unable to fulfill the Law. . . . Hence we are on the right way to salvation the moment we are convinced that we are ungodly." (See Romans 10:2–4.)

But by the grace of God I am what I am,
and His grace toward me was not in vain.
On the contrary, I worked harder than any of
them, though it was not I, but the grace of God
that is with me.

—1 Corinthians 15:10

CHAPTER 8

Becoming

We enter this world with the wrong identity. From the moment of conception, the identity we have is not the one God intended for us. As newborn infants, sin already has us in its grip so completely that we are corrupted with sin through and through. Our godless identity has been passed on to us through our ancestors, who were also sinners. It could correctly be said that we are all godless atheists on the day of our birth.

It could correctly be said that we are all godless atheists on the day of our birth.

We came into this world belonging to Satan. Had we been more fully developed physically, intellectually, and emotionally, we might have cursed God with our very first words. We resented the God who created us and has always loved us. When God said don't, our natural response was I'm going to do it anyway. When He said do, our tendency was to respond with I won't. We were like spoiled brats—rebellious, disobedient, willful—the kind of kids who embarrass their parents with their selfish tantrums and stubborn demands. In this condition, the only person who really matters is *me*.

Some people say the human race is more arrogant today than ever before. Culture watchers are expressing concern about our national dalliance with social narcissism and the absence of genuine humility. Author, commentator on culture and society, lecturer, and political pundit David Brooks writes:

> We have seen a broad shift from a culture of humility to the culture of what you might call the Big Me, from a culture that encouraged

> people to think humbly of themselves to a culture that encouraged people to see themselves as the center of the universe. . . . As I looked around the popular culture I kept finding the same messages everywhere: You are special. Trust yourself. Be true to yourself. Movies from Pixar and Disney are constantly telling children how wonderful they are. Commencement speeches are larded with the same clichés: Follow your passion. Don't accept limits. Chart your own course. You have a responsibility to do great things because you are so great. This is the gospel of self-trust. . . . Our basic problem is that we are self-centered. . . . This self-centeredness leads in several unfortunate directions. It leads to selfishness, the desire to use other people as a means to get things for yourself. It also leads to pride, the desire to see yourself as superior to everybody else.[1]

History teaches that the overreach that flows from arrogance often leads to unintended consequences. The attitude David Brooks describes above is dangerous because it bloats us and puffs us up on the psychological drugs of flattery, self-infatuation, and the dizzying spin of an inflated ego. This pipe-dream effect exposes a serious vulnerability.[2] Overreach invites disaster. Our enemies thrive when they discover that we are trapped in our own arrogance. Knowing who I am (my identity) demands the integrity of recognizing the weaknesses and flaws that limit what I can or cannot do. Moreover, the temptation to become so fully absorbed in our own earthly kingdoms can lead us to settle for earthly success in lieu of our eternal future. In other words, we are willing to squander the only opportunity for salvation we will ever have for a modicum of success in this temporary life, just to satiate our own narcissistic ego.[3] Jesus once asked His followers, "What will it profit a man if he gains the whole world and forfeits his soul? Or what shall a man give in return for his soul?" (Matthew 16:26). God's people should be asking this question every day.

Speaking of both children and adults, Martin Luther says, "[Baptism] indicates that the Old Adam in us should by daily contrition and repentance be drowned and die with all sins and evil desires, and that a new man should daily emerge and arise to live before God in righteousness and purity forever."[4] Such self-denial requires courage and the inner strength that comes from a faith that trusts God

1 Brooks, *Character*, 6–10.
2 See https://www.greekmyths-greekmythology.com/narcissus-myth-echo/.
3 See Matthew 19:16–30.
4 Small Catechism, Baptism, Fourth Part.

to provide all the resources that are needed to turn away from our own sinful inclinations.

Peter's overconfidence nearly cost him his eternal future. The very same night he vowed he would never deny his Lord, Peter, the rock of faith, swore an oath that he did not know Jesus. Years later, quoting from Proverbs 3:34, a much humbler Peter wrote, "Clothe yourselves, all of you, with humility toward one another, for 'God opposes the proud but gives grace to the humble' " (1 Peter 5:5).

In the early part of his career as a Jewish theologian, Paul had dedicated his life to persecuting Jews who followed Jesus. After his conversion, Paul could understand his identity only in the light of God's grace. In humble faith, he confessed, "By the grace of God I am what I am . . ." (1 Corinthians 15:10).

THE PROBLEM WITH COMPARING

It is inherent in human beings to compare ourselves with other human beings. This can be a wonderful blessing. For example, we are doubly blessed to see how Jesus conducted His life on earth. Becoming Christlike is a God-pleasing objective for Christians. But comparing ourselves to others isn't always a godly choice. In a sinful world, the impulse to compare can also be driven by arrogance and pride.

Jesus knows the temptations we face. He experienced Satan's assaults firsthand. He knows that we sometimes shamefully indulge in comparing ourselves with others in order to create the impression that we are morally superior. This kind of comparing is wrong because it is fundamentally dishonest. In God's eyes, we are all guilty of sin. The verdict that demands punishment for our wrongdoing is not a burden we must bear because our divine Judge is a mean God. It is because He is a just God, and His justice is perfect.

God does not want us to judge the motives of other people. Jesus warned, "Judge not, that you be not judged. For with the judgment you pronounce you will be judged, and with the measure you use it will be measured to you" (Matthew 7:1–2). God has not given human beings the capacity to know what goes on in the hearts of others. Heeding Jesus' warning is in our own best interest.

On the other hand, the Son of God was Himself not completely opposed to the practice of making comparisons. When it came to comparing people's faith, our Lord Jesus—the Judge of all mankind—made some startling observations that were based on His divine insights.

THE QUEST FOR GREAT FAITH

A centurion came to Jesus to intervene on behalf of his servant, who was suffering at home with a debilitating paralysis. The condition was terminal. The servant was in dire pain. When Jesus promised to come to the centurion's house to heal the servant, the centurion replied, "Lord, I am not worthy to have You come under my roof, but only say the word, and my servant will be healed" (Matthew 8:8).

The centurion was not a Jew, and Jesus was amazed by his confession. He said so publicly. "Truly, I tell you, with no one in Israel have I found such faith" (v. 10). The servant was healed within the hour.

The disciples were taking notes.[5] The topic of great faith was bound to be revisited.

One night, Jesus and some of His disciples were crossing the Sea of Galilee. A squall came up while Jesus slept. When the wind and waves threatened to capsize the boat, the disciples became so afraid that they awakened Jesus. Before He quieted the storm and calmed the waves, the Master asked them why their faith was so weak (Matthew 8:23–27).

Surely, the Master's question bothered His students.

Another dark night on the Sea of Galilee, when Jesus was not with His disciples, they thought they saw a ghost hovering over the water (Matthew 14:22–31). Peter realized the specter was actually his dear Rabbi. Impulsively, Peter jumped out of the boat and began walking on top of the water toward Jesus. It was an amazing example of faith, until Peter had second thoughts. Suddenly, his faith didn't seem so remarkable, and he started to sink. Fearing he was about to die, Peter cried out, "Lord, save me" (v. 30).

Jesus stretched out His hand to save Peter from drowning. Back in the boat, He looked Peter in the eye and asked, "O you of little faith, why did you doubt?" (v. 31).

Peter had failed the faith test. It wouldn't be the last time.

A Canaanite woman came to Jesus, asking for help. Her daughter was suffering from demon possession. Jesus tested the woman's faith, suggesting He could not help her because she was not a Jew. When the woman said she would be happy to receive the scraps of blessings that fell from the Jews' table, Jesus complimented her faith and healed her daughter (Matthew 15:21–28).

The disciples wondered why Jesus had never complimented *their* faith.

One day, a man brought his epileptic son to Jesus. The boy was demon possessed. The boy's father explained that his son would fall into the fire or slip into a pond, putting his life and the lives of others at risk. The boy's father had actually come the previous day, asking the disciples for help. They were not able to cure the

5 The disciples struggled with the question of who had the greatest faith during most of the time that they were Jesus' students. They began to understand the connection between faith and humility after Jesus' ascension.

boy. After Jesus rebuked the demon and healed the boy, the disciples asked Him privately, "Why could we not cast it out?" (Matthew 17:19). "Because of your little faith," replied Jesus (v. 20).

The Master's remark was undoubtedly a devastating blow to their egos.

When the disciples discussed faith among themselves, the dialogue usually degenerated into a debate about who was the greatest in God's kingdom. Finally, one of them found the courage to ask Jesus, "Who is the greatest in the kingdom of heaven?" (Matthew 18:1).

AN OBJECT LESSON

Jesus knew about the tensions this question raised among His followers. The issue had finally culminated in this teachable moment (Matthew 18:1–4). The Master was not about to pass up the opportunity.[6]

Calling a young child into the room, the Rabbi invited His followers to study the lad closely. Jesus wanted His disciples to compare their adult worldviews with the worldviews of this child. It's likely that He wanted them to remember their own childhoods. He wanted them to note how much their worldview had changed since they were young.

"Truly, I say to you," began Jesus, "unless you turn and become like children, you will never enter the kingdom of heaven. Whoever humbles himself like this child is the greatest in the kingdom of heaven" (vv. 3–4).

One can only assume that the disciples were stunned. They knew their teacher wanted them to learn a spiritual truth. But this lesson was hardly reassuring. Words such as "unless" and "never" must have been distressing terms when coupled with the promise of heaven and the resurrection from the dead. Was their Lord really saying that if they failed to become childlike, they would not have eternal life? Did He really mean that something within them had to change?

Jesus talked often about the kingdom with His disciples. They were familiar with some of the great civilizations of the past—Assyrians, Egyptians, Babylonians, Persians, Greeks, the hated Romans. They understood that human kingdoms lasted only for a while and then flamed out.

Some of us invest our lives building our own earthly kingdoms in areas of human endeavors such as medicine, education, commerce, agriculture, finance, the trades, technology, law enforcement, or the military. We call these earthly kingdoms our careers. Other people choose to construct their personal kingdoms

6 Galstad, *Findings*, 100–101. Galstad wrote, "Jesus looked for fruit from his disciples. What they were was not much cause for rejoicing at the time, but he called them friends—in the hope, we can be sure, of what they would become. The mere 'son of John' became Peter the rock. Thomas the doubter became the confessor. If that which was dust became a living soul, don't stop at what a child is, but keep in mind what he can become."

around their ego, legacy, personal influence, wealth, authority, talent, status, even family. We all know people who have dedicated every waking moment of their lives pursuing the lifelong dream they have constructed around one of these earthly kingdoms. But, at what cost?

The youngster standing there before the Twelve was thoroughly unmoved by the struggles and stresses of earthly kingdoms. It's fair to guess that he had no aspirations for a career in kingdom building. Nor did he have anything to offer for securing such a future—no PhD, pedigree, social status, Swiss bank account, political clout, influence, résumé, title, VIP connections, venture capital, or stellar reputation. Matthew did not even bother to record the child's name. This little guy likely was a nobody, a nothing. Yet, one can imagine that like most children, he lived every day to the full, falling into bed at night exhausted from his day's playful activities. Happy and carefree. His humility would have been pure and unforced. Without ever thinking about how, or why, anyone would bother to take care of him, the youngster was delighted with his dependent status and unconcerned about his daily sustenance. Life was good. God was good. The child would have trusted his parents to meet all of his needs. And they did. The child was a living picture of simple trust—a metaphor for the kind of faith that boldly follows in the Savior's footsteps without ever bothering to wonder where, or from whom, all those wonderful blessings were coming. In profound humility, this youngster would have known that God blessed him every day.

The child likely touched the disciples' hearts. In response to this object lesson, one can imagine how each man tried to recall his own childhood, when there were no expectations for greatness, success, or achievement. The only demands were immediate. Be good. Listen. Obey. Life as a child was uncomplicated, uncluttered, unencumbered. Kingdom building was the farthest thing from his youthful thoughts.

A lot had changed since Jesus' followers had become grown-ups. They had needs that had to be met. Some of them had families. Their worldview was an adult's worldview. Some were driven by their own dreams, while others were satisfied merely to survive. Those who had some luck along the way, or the courage to fight for their place in the sun, might someday have a chance to grab the brass ring. But glory of that kind is rare. It lasts only so long. The temptation to forget that all we have comes from God is quite universal among adults. It is a constant threat to one's faith in God's providence.

The notion that an adult could somehow become childlike remained a deep mystery to Jesus' disciples. We all eventually become adults. It might be prolonged, but such change can never be fully curtailed. And once an individual has arrived at adulthood, there's no turning back. If it had not been their beloved Master who uttered this outrageous notion, the whole idea would have seemed ludicrous. As it was, none of them had ever heard of anything so ridiculous as an adult who had miraculously returned to that sublime life stage when life was so unfettered.

We are God's dependents.

In time, the disciples began to realize this was the whole point of Jesus' lesson. Becoming childlike was never going to happen for these grown men. Not in a million years! Not without the intervention of someone with superhuman power. They were doomed to reside in the limited kingdoms of their adult world, in the bubble of adult striving and earthbound kingdom building. Short of some kind of miracle, they would never escape.

Becoming childlike has the same challenges for us. The only way it can happen is if an almighty and loving God intervenes, not by turning back the clock, but by transforming our adult worldview and the focus of our self-sufficient hearts to total trust that He will keep every one of His promises. We are God's dependents. We are completely reliant on God's generous, daily blessings. We have absolutely nothing to offer in compensation for them. If we are totally honest, we have no choice but to trust God to provide all that we need for this life and beyond. I AM's grace intervenes. We may have started life with the wrong identity, but God stepped in. He replaced our godless identity with the new understanding that now we are His own dear children, members of His holy family, and heirs to His throne.

THE HUMBLEST

Into this battleground of despair came the King of intervention. But He didn't look like royalty when He arrived. Nor did He resemble a conquering hero. Christ became the ultimate picture of humility by leaving His throne in God's heavenly kingdom to take on human flesh. In a miracle no human mind can comprehend, Jesus became both God and man at the same time. The extremes that distinguished the divine Creator from His human creatures were in Christ's being. In Him, we find both glory and humility at their zenith. Yet, they were never in conflict. He was, is, and always will be God. For us, He entered the dimensions of time, space, and change through His mother's birth canal, into a world where human beings live and the world He Himself had created. He was exactly the kind of human being God intended His human creatures should be when God first created them in Eden. Our holy God, who abhors sin, humbled Himself to become human. As Paul puts it, "For our sake He [God] made Him [Jesus] to be sin who knew no sin, so that in Him we might become the righteousness of God" (2 Corinthians 5:21).

HIS WORK AND OURS

Jesus took on human flesh to finish the work the Trinity began when the universe was created. He did it to set humankind free from the enslaving chains of sin, death, and the devil's grip on people's lives. He became a humble servant to His human creatures, those creatures who from birth rejected Him and dismissed His work. He kept God's Law perfectly, because for sinners such absolute perfection was impossible. He did it to take upon Himself the punishment we deserved so that we would not spend eternity in the godlessness of hell. He did it to empower us to live in humble obedience to the heavenly Father's will. Jesus' work perfectly completes everything God requires for our salvation.

When He left this earth to return to His throne in heaven, King Jesus called us into His service as co-workers, commissioning us to carry His work forward. Paul brought these Bible truths together around the simple theme of humility.

> Have this mind among yourselves, which is yours in Christ Jesus, who, though He was in the form of God, did not count equality with God a thing to be grasped, but emptied Himself, by taking the form of a servant, being born in the likeness of men. And being found in human form, He humbled Himself by becoming obedient to the point of death, even death on a cross. (Philippians 2:5–8)

[Father,] I have given them Your word, and the world has hated them because they are not of the world, just as I am not of the world. I do not ask that You take them out of the world, but that You keep them from the evil one. They are not of the world, just as I am not of the world. Sanctify them in the truth; Your word is truth.

—John 17:14–17

CHAPTER 9

A Two-Kingdom Lens

God distinguished humankind with the intellectual capacity to think complex thoughts, render useful observations, and remember volumes of data. In terms of their capacity to think, children are intellectual wizards. They begin to construct their own worldview at a very early age. By the end of their second year, children have accumulated a vocabulary of about one thousand words. They can organize words in ordered sequence (nouns and verbs) to communicate complete and meaningful thoughts. Early conversations are mostly one-sided and one-word soliloquies, but it doesn't take long for a child to discover that other people can be engaged when they ask questions. Suddenly, every thought begins with the most important word in every two-year-old's vocabulary: *Why?*

The answers to why the heavenly Father created us; why His Son redeemed us from sin, death, and the devil's power; and why His Spirit gives us the gift of faith all point to the most powerful force known to humankind: God's love.

Children instinctively grasp that knowing why is the key to their understanding of the universe. Their insatiable thirst for such knowledge is also the key to survival in a dangerous world. Knowing why leads to an understanding of those forces that cause things to happen in their ever-changing environment. Answers to the word *why* have the potential to take a child's understanding to an intellectual level that is more interested in exploring causes than simple facts.

All this is reason enough to be thankful for the ravenous curiosity that won't let our kids stop asking why. But knowing why is also the key to understanding our relationship with God. The answers to why the heavenly Father created us; why His Son redeemed us from sin, death, and the devil's power; and why His Spirit gives us the gift of faith all point to the most powerful force known to humankind: God's love.[1] Why did God perform in these most wonderful ways? Because He loves us.

KNOWING, IN THE BEGINNING

Some Bible experts have theorized that the first human beings possessed a superior human intellect. The Bible neither confirms nor contests this theory. Adam certainly appreciated the love his Creator expressed to him in the daily blessings God provided. Like a child, Adam must have been eager to learn how he fit into his surroundings. He must have wanted to know more about the role God had given him. He must have been curious about how to harness his intellectual abilities to fulfill his God-given role. He must have wondered where he could find human companionship.

God had a plan to help Adam acquire valuable knowledge about his environment. He prepared Adam for his first encounter with another human being. Adam would be all the more grateful for a human companion when he understood the blessings he would be missing without one. God's plan was to let Adam exercise his intellect by becoming a scientist. Adam needed to learn how to learn. To accomplish this, God assigned Adam the task of assigning a name to all the living creatures in Eden. Names apparently matter even for animals.

Adam used the same technique science uses today; he learned by observation. When he compared the animals to himself, he discovered that, in moral terms, he was like God with respect to his moral rightness. None of the other creatures in the garden possessed God's righteous image. They were amoral creatures. He noticed, too, that no other animals possessed his advanced intellect.

We learn the same way Adam learned. We gather information, observe, and make logical comparisons. Unlike Adam, we have the added advantage of being able to get our information second- or thirdhand from those who have gathered new data from their own experience. According to one poet, we all learn by standing on the shoulders of giants.

There are a few things we do not know, should not know, or cannot know. With the exception of knowing that my eternal future will be spent with Jesus in the new creation, I know only a handful of vague details that the Bible tells

---

1 A brief study of spiritual knowledge might include the following readings: Job 19:25; Proverbs 2; John 2:20–25; 3:11; 4:42; 9:25; 10:14; 17:3; 1 Corinthians 8:3; 13:12; 2 Timothy 1:8–12; 2 Peter 1:3–8.

me about the eternal future that waits for me there.[2] Moreover, there are many things mentioned in the Bible that we just don't understand. Here's the point: The notion that there are no limits to the human mind's growth potential is a myth. The human capacity to grow intellectually has defined boundaries that begin with the simple truth that God is God and we are not. (That simple truth is exactly what the people of Babel needed to learn.)

The human capacity to grow intellectually has defined boundaries that begin with the simple truth that God is God and we are not.

MORE THAN ONE WAY OF KNOWING

People have the capacity to embrace knowledge in a number of ways. This is because there are different kinds of knowledge, including the recall of academic facts, mystical knowing, and innovative thought. Some knowledge is intuitive. Intuition utilizes the things we already know, without having first to learn them. For example, without instruction, babies instinctively seem to know the significance of a smile. They experience joy when they see someone smile at them. It is probably a smile that acknowledges a human relationship. People intuitively seem to know there is a second (transcendent) kingdom. Scripture supports this observation.[3]

Most of the things we know are learned. We use our senses to see, hear, taste, smell, and feel in order to learn more about those elements in our environment that hold our attention. The information we collect is organized into systems and broken down into logical relationships—cause and effect, first and last, him and her, and so on. The information is then stored for further use.

We hear God giving instructions to Noah for building an ark. Use gopher wood; be precise about the dimensions; construct it with three decks; put a door on one side (Genesis 6:13–16). It was up to Noah and the other members of his family to work their way through God's basic sketch and come up with a plan for implementing His instructions. New tools had to be invented. Someone had to think about where to build, how to position the timbers for the ark's keel, how to erect a four-story superstructure. They had to acquire knowledge about torque, leverage, gravity, and the physics of water pressure. None of this was particularly intuitive. It would require effort, study, thought, and new learning curves.

2 For a brief study of the end times, consider Matthew 24:3–51; 28:20; Hebrews 9:26; 1 Thessalonians 5:2; 2 Peter 3:10.

3 See Romans 1:20; Psalm 97:6–7.

In 1995, Daniel Goleman challenged the notion that intellectual thought was the only kind of knowing. Goleman proposed an emotion-based kind of knowing that he called emotional intelligence (EI). He described emotional intelligence as "self-control, zeal and persistence, and the ability to motivate oneself" and "being able . . . to rein in emotional impulse; to read another's innermost feelings; to handle relationships smoothly."[4]

In general, and not in a scientific sense, the Bible seems to support the notion of emotional intelligence. For example, Noah and his family demonstrated a kind of emotional intelligence when they gave thanks for God's deliverance from the flood.

The whole idea of offering an animal sacrifice as their first act after stepping off the ark seems a bit counterintuitive. There must have been a thousand other things that needed their attention. Yet, an irrepressible impulse led them to express their appreciation to God in this special way. Their decision to sacrifice an animal first, before doing anything else, seems to have been driven less by knowledge, or even instinct, than by the powerful emotion of gratitude.

Need more biblical evidence to support the notion of EI?

Love—so difficult to define, and even more elusive to deal with in a logical way—is a good example. We all have a general sense of what love looks like in real life. Paul actually described godly behaviors connected to the emotion of love. His divinely inspired taxonomy (some stated in the negative) noted fifteen specific virtue-driven behaviors.[5] Here is the apostle's explanation of how the abstract emotion of love transforms lovers (their identity) into performers (what they do) by giving substance to their feelings through virtuous human actions and behaviors.

> Love is patient and kind; love does not envy or boast; it is not arrogant or rude. It does not insist on its own way; it is not irritable or resentful; it does not rejoice at wrongdoing, but rejoices with the truth. Love bears all things, believes all things, hopes all things, endures all things. (1 Corinthians 13:4–7)

Goleman's ideas generated a lot of attention. The concept may have set a whole series of cultural shifts in motion. These trends tended to place more emphasis on exploring whatever is meant by terms such as "loving behaviors." Science, true

4 Daniel Goleman, *Emotional Intelligence: Why It Can Matter More Than IQ* (New York: Bantam Books, 1995), xii, xiii. Goleman's definition for emotional intelligence (EI) was actually developed by Michael Beldoch thirty years earlier for a journal article.

5 Note how Paul's taxonomy comes close to many of the virtues listed in *Appendix B: Biblical Character*—behaviors such as patience, kindness, unselfishness, humility, respect, selflessness, peace-loving, forgiving, honesty, compassion, hopefulness, and perseverance.

to form, also reacted with a flurry of new theories. But two decades of intense study raised doubts about some of Goleman's constructs. Today, science generally views emotional knowing as just another way of gathering new information. Meanwhile, the unscientific community's response to EI has been something like this: didn't we already know that emotional intelligence existed?

These multiple ways of understanding our world of time, space, and change are tailor made for helping us carry out our responsibilities as good stewards of God's earthly kingdom. In the stewardship role, people of godly character care deeply about exercising wisdom, self-discipline, and self-restraint in caring for our planet. And there's a lot to know if we are going to do a good job of fulfilling the obligations of our God-given role. Our time and energy should be spent learning about our environment. There is even a certain nobility to gathering knowledge about our present reality. Responsible science leads to discovery and invention. Knowing the facts of history helps us understand human progress and divine faithfulness. Math courses teach us how to measure the world we live in so we can respect real limits to human endeavor. Art envisions new realities through the mind's eye of imagination. Literature expands horizons by giving people the opportunity to explore relationships through the written word.

Welcome to the world of education.

We not only need to learn how to navigate our environments, but we also need to learn how to get along with one another—to share, trust, instruct, encourage, forgive, support. God's Word tells us to love our neighbors *and* our enemies. Learning to love one's enemies can place us on a perilous learning curve. Honoring and respecting the legitimate authority of sinful people, whether they be friend or foe, can sometimes feel like an impossible mission.

When some Pharisees asked Jesus what He thought of paying taxes to a brutal and corrupt Roman government, He pointed to a Roman coin and asked, "Whose likeness and inscription is this?" When they answered, "Caesar's," Jesus said, "Render to Caesar the things that are Caesar's, and to God the things that are God's" (Matthew 22:20–22).

The ethic Jesus was teaching was an extension of the Fourth Commandment, one of the commandments that focuses on our human relationships: "Honor your father and your mother, as the LORD your God commanded you, that your days may be long, and that it may go well with you in the land that the LORD your God is giving you" (Deuteronomy 5:16).[6] We are to respect and honor those with whom God has shared some of His authority. They are to use that authority to protect and defend us, to maintain law and order in our society, to lead and

---

6 A brief study of the biblical ethic of honoring and obeying authority could include Matthew 22:21; Ephesians 6:1–3; Hebrews 13:7, 17; 1 Peter 2:13–17; Romans 13:1–7.

encourage. Embedded in Jesus' lesson is a hidden exhortation to thank God for blessing us with leaders at the national, state, and local levels. As citizens of earthly kingdoms, giving honor includes paying taxes, serving when called upon to protect our nation's people, and giving voice to our concerns as the opportunity presents. These are compelling moral expectations for the citizens of this world's earthly kingdoms. And, yes, this ethic includes giving honor and respect to heartless tyrants, ineffective do-nothings, irresponsible lawmakers, and poor decision makers. In His time, God will judge them on the basis of His Law and the spiritual condition of their hearts. He also wants us to honor and respect individuals who lead in other venues—parents, church leaders, law enforcement, judges, pastors, and teachers.[7] In our era, it is getting hard to find much honor or respect for people who are filling roles of authority.[8] As with all moral judgments, the line between honorable and disgraceful is in the intent. Sin begins in the heart. People who take these words from God's Law to heart lead virtuous lives as they strive to obey every facet of the Fourth Commandment.

This is a good spot in our conversation to remind ourselves that earthly kingdoms need good schools. Businesses, farms, and factories need reliable workers. Institutions—that is, the military, law enforcement, hospitals, banks, law firms—need people who are committed to their respective professions and possess the skills, attitudes, and knowledge to carry out their work that benefits society. In each of these occupations, integrity is a given.

Public education is an essential component of our particular kind of social structure. Public schools help hold communities together. They teach young people to be productive citizens. They instill in our children cultural norms that stress noble ideals such as equality, unity, diversity, freedom, integrity, loyalty, right to peaceful dissent, the rule of law, and so on. We owe a debt of gratitude to the men and women who teach children, coach children, correct children, and care for children. On a regular basis, we pray for them and the success of their work.

We also need to express honor and respect for Christian people who teach in the public sector. Their jobs are not easy. The truths that must be articulated to expose the underlying godless moral foundations of secular education must never be allowed to detract from or disparage the efforts of those God-fearing individuals who labor in secular schools. These people quietly provide models of the godly life to their students, even when the law forbids them from teaching the tenets of their faith in public classrooms.

---

7 *Luther's Small Catechism with Explanation*, Question 54.

8 Hunter, *Death*, 191. "A moral code that is, at bottom, self-generating and self-referencing undermines the existence of and adherence to a prevailing communal purpose; it precludes the possibility of any compelling collective discipline capable of regulating social life. Simply put, there is nothing to which the self is obligated to submit."

KNOWING BY FAITH

There is another kind of knowing that stretches our horizon from the here and now of earthly kingdoms to a reality as infinite as God Himself. This kind of knowledge not only engages the human mind, but also brings life and light to the soul. It has an extremely powerful lens that focuses narrowly on one sublime truth that Christ Jesus loves me and died to make me His own child. Such knowledge exclusively flows from a biblical frame. It is called *faith*, and is also referred to as "trust," "conviction," or "belief." Faith is a deeply personal kind of knowing; we might think of it as "my truth."[9] The Bible speaks of faith as being very precious. It is speaking of saving faith in Jesus. As one preacher put it, "Our faith is established by the testimony of God Himself. And because it is God's Word, it is able to make [us] wise unto salvation through faith in Jesus Christ. . . . That Word testifies not only of what God says and promises, but of what He's done. It's a testimony of God's action."[10] This is an important point because everyone, believer and unbeliever alike, has faith in someone or something.

The Bible speaks of faith as being very precious.

Knowing by faith is what happened in the heart of the dying thief when Jesus said he would enter God's kingdom that very day. Suddenly, unexpectedly, the man knew Jesus' heart. He knew, through the lens of faith, that his own heart now belonged to Jesus. He knew his salvation was at hand. He knew peace and joy. He knew the reality of God and His kingdom. In these waning moments of his life, the man may not have been able to conceptualize his future home, but he believed that the reality Jesus had just promised to him meant a new life. He knew it was a gift—neither earned nor deserved. And what he knew made him cling all the more to Jesus' promise. The thief's faith changed his entire outlook on his wicked past and his painful present. This was his new life in Christ. It refocused his new worldview on his joyous, eternal future.

Such hopeful knowledge changes us too. It turns a heart careening down the highway to hell into a heart that trusts in God's eternal kingdom. Faith changes one's worldview, causing an individual to want to live in obedience to God's will. It turns ordinary character into godly character. It replaces our hatred for God with a deep and abiding love for Him. Faith begins to restore the image of God that was lost when Adam and Eve fell into sin. Where unbelief desperately strives to acquire more from their earthly realities, God's people of faith spend themselves

9 See Hebrews 11:1.

10 From "Faith Is . . . (Hebrews 11:1–16)," a sermon delivered by Wayne Braun on August 7, 2016, at Trinity Lutheran Church, Frankfurt am Mein, Germany, accessed August 16, 2016, https://soundcloud.com/trinity-frankfurt/080716-faith-ismp3 080716 MP3.

hopefully begging God to give them more faith to live in faithful gratitude by giving all glory to their God of hope.

Faith is not acquired in the same way that other knowledge is acquired. It comes to us without any effort on our part. In fact, faith comes to us in spite of our natural resistance to it. It comes to us by the divine power of the Holy Spirit.

Faith is not acquired in the same way that other knowledge is acquired. It comes to us without any effort on our part. In fact, faith comes to us in spite of our natural resistance to it. It comes to us by the divine power of the Holy Spirit. His spiritual energy can actually change the wretched condition of a sinful human heart. The power of God's Word and the Sacraments connected to that Word are His tools of the trade. These tools are dedicated solely to our spiritual transformation. No other power on earth can make that claim.

OLD TESTAMENT EXAMPLES OF LIVING FAITH

Noah and his family knew the promises of God were reliable. Their trust in God's promise to send a flood moved them to build an ark on dry land—in the face of social isolation and ridicule.

When Abraham still lived in Mesopotamia, God told him to move his family to a place where he would one day receive his promised inheritance. Though he did not know where he was going, Abraham obeyed. God led Abraham and his family to their new home in a foreign land—a place called Canaan (modern-day Israel)—where they lived in tents because they did not own land of their own. Abraham's son Isaac and his grandson Jacob received the same promises from God. They, too, lived in tents and lived the nomadic life. Yet, by faith, they foresaw a time when they would live in a city that had solid foundations, whose architect and builder was God.[11] Here's how the New Testament writer of Hebrews finished the story.

> These all died in faith, not having received the things promised, but having seen them and greeted them from afar, and having acknowledged that they were strangers and exiles on the earth. For people who speak thus make it clear that they are seeking a homeland. If they had been thinking of that land from which they had gone out, they would have had opportunity to return. But as it is, they de-

11 A description of "the city of the living God" that Abraham envisioned is recorded in Hebrews 12:22–24.

> sire a better country, that is, a heavenly one. Therefore God is not ashamed to be called their God, for He has prepared for them a city. (Hebrews 11:13–16)

A HEAVENLY VIEW

Call it a city, a kingdom, a homeland, or the Promised Land. Whatever we call it, the goal of our faith has already been achieved, just as it had been achieved for Abraham, Isaac, Jacob, and their families. Eternal life is our future, and we already possess God's sure promise of that secure future right now, in this life.

The technical term for the study of the end times, the judgment, and the eternal destiny of the soul is *eschatology*. This study describes the Christian's life as having one foot planted in the temporary soil of this world's kingdoms, while the other foot is anchored in the permanent and eternal security of God's heavenly kingdom. Christian character has an eschatological worldview firmly embedded in its narrative. That narrative always ends with a new and better genesis for God's people. We nurture the faith of future generations by giving them the same hope for their future that we have, namely the promise of the resurrection from the dead.

Christian character has an eschatological worldview firmly embedded in its narrative.

Stanley Hauerwas, a widely read Christian philosopher and author, considered the importance of having an eschatological frame of mind. Hauerwas wrote:

> To begin to understand Jesus' announcement of the kingdom, we must first rid ourselves of the notion that the world we experience will exist indefinitely. We must learn to see the world as Israel had learned to understand it—that is, eschatologically. Though it sounds powerful and intimidating, in fact it is quite simple, for to view the world eschatologically is to see it in terms of a story, with a beginning, a continuing drama, and an end. . . . It is against this background that Jesus' announcement of the kingdom must be seen, for he came to announce an end that, while not yet final, nonetheless provided a necessary perspective for our continuing life in the world.[12]

For the believer and unbeliever alike, there are some temporary pleasures to be enjoyed in this life—special memories and wonderful relationships, exciting

12 Hauerwas, *Peaceable Kingdom*, 82.

For those who trust in God's promises, faith clings to the hope for the coming reality.

adventures, learning opportunities. In the long run, however, our earthly reality is largely a kingdom of heartache, disappointment, suffering, and correction, even for the believer, especially for the believer. The unbeliever's lens is clouded by the concerns of this life, made only worse by the prospect that one must still eventually face the inevitability of death. The unbeliever's view is limited to the time, space, and changing environments of this present reality. For those who trust in God's promises, faith clings to the hope for the coming reality. His people look forward to a new creation, where "good" is a return to the perfect wonder of Eden and a secure relationship with our loving God. We know the rest of our story. We know how it ends—that is, with no end, but rather the end of godlessness and rebellion, when God's holy image will be fully restored to us.[13]

In this life, we are nomads, living in a foreign land in the flimsy tents of our bodies that grow old and succumb to injuries, sickness, and disease. Yet, our faith is constantly pulling us heavenward, even as we remain temporarily tethered to this life. The spiritual knowledge of faith is the most precious thing we own. It is the window through which we are able to see what is waiting for us.

THE NOW AND THE THEN OF LIFE

This eschatological view, in which the eyes of godly people are fixed on Jesus and their worldview's gaze is trained heavenward, gives believers a two-dimensional understanding of life that is not part of the unbeliever's spiritual vocabulary. God's language of faith is nonsense to the unbeliever. For the believer, that faith changes everything because it sees life as a two-dimensional reality. Paul summarizes the eschatological aspect of a Christian's faith like this.

> As for prophecies, they will pass away; as for tongues, they will cease; as for knowledge, it will pass away. For we know in part and we prophesy in part, but when the perfect comes, the partial will pass away. When I was a child, I spoke like a child, I thought like a child, I reasoned like a child. When I became a man, I gave up childish ways. For now we see in a mirror dimly, but then face to face. Now I know in part; then I shall know fully, even as I have been fully known. (1 Corinthians 13:8–12)

---

13 In 1 John 3:2, we are told, "We are God's children now, and what we will be has not yet appeared; but we know that when He appears we shall be like Him, because we shall see Him as He is."

Today, we know God's truth imperfectly as we remain in the temporary reality of *now*. *Then* we will understand God's faithfulness to its fullest measure as we enter the perfection of His eternal kingdom.

Keeping one eye on the then of eternity and the other eye on the now of a growing family or a struggling business is not easy.

But Paul's description of then takes an abrupt turn as the spotlight shifts from what I know in faith right now to the simple object of my faith, Jesus. The most beautiful thing about my faith is in knowing that I am known by my loving, heavenly Father. He loves me. Nothing could stop Him from doing everything necessary to make it possible for me to spend eternity with Him. Though he did not know what outcome he was seeking, this is what the thief had been praying for when he begged Jesus to remember him. He wanted to be significant in the eyes of God. Knowing God is huge. Being known and loved by God is even better, because being known by God Himself is where the real joy of a new genesis begins.

Living with a two-kingdom worldview is a challenge. Keeping one eye on the then of eternity and the other eye on the now of a growing family or a struggling business is not easy. Yet, God uses our "now and then" lens to keep the hope in our heavenly future alive. He uses it to change our thinking about life so that it begins to align with His worldview. By seeing both now and then through the two-dimensional lens of faith means that we are already straddling both kingdoms.

For in Christ Jesus neither circumcision
nor uncircumcision counts for anything,
but only faith working through love.

—Galatians 5:6

CHAPTER 10

Two Kinds of Righteousness

Martin Luther's understanding of what it means to be human focused on two special kinds of relationships. The first is the relationship we have with God. The second focus is found in the relationships we have with our fellow human beings. From Scripture, Luther knew that all sinners have access to a loving relationship with God through faith in Jesus. He also saw that having a restored relationship with God changes our relationships with the people around us. Luther came to understand that these two kinds of relationships were intimately connected and that humankind was designed to find enjoyment and meaning in them both.

In their book *The Genius of Luther's Theology*, Robert Kolb and Charles Arand note that Luther referred to these two dimensions as "the two kinds of righteousness." The first kind of righteousness is in relationship to faith; the second is in relationship to love. Luther's approach explains how these two Spirit-driven forces—one in which God's people are passive and the other in which we are actively reaching out in love to the world around us—gives substance to our new spiritual being.[1] Kolb and Arand write,

> To be righteous is to be the human person God envisioned when he created us. It has to do with meeting God's "design specifications"

1 Our new spiritual being is our "new man in Christ," our Christian identity.

for being a human creature and fulfilling the purpose for which God created us.[2]

The ability to actually do good works for others is really a very special blessing.

Passages such as Ephesians 2:8–10 stunned Luther by laying out God's plan for His people in clear and simple terms: "For by grace you have been saved through faith. And this is not your own doing; it is the gift of God, not a result of works, so that no one may boast. For we are His workmanship, created in Christ Jesus for good works, which God prepared beforehand, that we should walk in them." As God's full plan began to emerge for Luther, he saw that the love emanating from God is what drives our performance. Moreover, it drives the good works that involve us in serving others. The ability to actually do good works for others is really a very special blessing. Christlike love diminishes the focus we have on ourselves and sharpens our focus on the needs of others. Our new character begins to think and behave more like Jesus. So does our desire to give instead of take. With this renewed worldview, Jesus' parable of the Good Samaritan encourages believers, in their everyday walk of faith, to let their light shine among the people they touch with God's love.

Sin takes. It took a perfect relationship and a perfect garden away from Adam and Eve. It took the image of God away from humankind, and with it, the perfect relationship between the Creator and His human creatures. Sin takes our health, our youth, our lives. It is only natural, then, that sinful people are inclined to spend a lifetime taking.

Love gives.[3]

In an interesting little book entitled *Listen! God Is Calling: Luther Speaks of Vocation, Faith, and Work*, D. Michael Bennethum explains that our loving focus on the everyday needs of others is the main element in Luther's teaching of vocation. Bennethum writes,

> The teaching on vocation, as articulated by Martin Luther and other reformers in the 16th century . . . is rooted in the confidence that God, the Creator, is still at work in and through the structures of daily life. It encourages workers to notice how their activities benefit their neighbors and thereby have value in the eyes of God. It

2 Kolb and Arand, *Genius*, 26.

3 Kolb and Arand, *Genius*, 126–27. "Faith produces new desires, attitudes, and dispositions to align one's life with God's design; new willingness to cooperate with God; recognition and gratitude for his many gifts, in both creation and redemption. Faith awakens character traits and may even free those character traits from their bondage to the flesh." (See Philippians 2:3–4, 7; Galatians 5:13; John 13:5.)

> endeavors to overcome the gulf between the sacred and the secular by understanding all of life as an expression of faith.[4]

Faith overcomes unbelief. It also begins to transform our wayward formula for character that, in sin, became stubborn and rebellious. With faith in Jesus, our reformed equation looks increasingly more like **C = I + P**. Our attitudes, activities, and general focus in life reflects the power of Jesus' love working in our lives and through us into the lives of others.

The connection between faith and love is almost seamless. In their union, we begin to perform like one would expect a child of God to perform.

With faith in Jesus, our reformed equation looks increasingly more like C = I + P.

So far, we have generally referred to our new identity as being "a child of God." This is a great starting point for understanding who we are. It is also a wonderful concept to introduce to young children when you are explaining their spiritual identity to them. As a child of God, children can readily begin to understand that their broken relationship with their loving heavenly Father has been fully restored by Jesus' redemptive work. It marks them as members of God's dear family of believers and heirs of His kingdom.

We have also explored the identity we inherited from Jacob, whose name God changed to Israel—the "One Who Wrestled with God." This identity also provides a teachable moment for children as they begin to think about the challenges of living in a sinful world, where adversity, disappointment, temptation, and heartache will be a real part of their lives. But the Bible refers to a few other ways to identify ourselves as being "in Christ." It's time to get acquainted with some of the other facets of the new you.

TASTE AND SEE

Jesus applied the special I AM name that God had revealed to Moses. John recorded these references in his Gospel. "I am the bread of life," said Jesus. "I am the light of the world." "I am the gate to heaven." "I am the way." "I am the resurrection and the life."[5] Each time Jesus identified with that I AM name, His disciples were forced to see the divine connection between Jesus and the true God they

---

4 D. Michael Bennethum, *Listen! God Is Calling: Luther Speaks of Vocation, Faith, and Work* (Minneapolis: Augsburg Fortress, 2003), 39.

5 For a brief study of Jesus' "I am" statements, see John 4:26; 6:35; 8:23, 58; 9:5; 10:7, 36; 11:25; 13:13; 14:6; 15:1; Revelation 1:8, 17.

worshiped. As the end of Jesus' ministry on earth approached, He was spelling out His divine connection as the Son of God to them in no uncertain terms.[6]

In a sermon recorded in John 15:5, Jesus looked each of His followers in the eye and gave us all a new name. "I am the vine; you are the branches. Whoever abides in Me and I in him, he it is that bears much fruit, for apart from Me you can do nothing." The vine and branches name not only tells us who we are, but it also explains our relationship with Him. He nurtures; we grow. Perhaps you can picture the two of you together, smiling, arm-in-arm, standing in front of the big wooden doors of God's sacred winery. You point to the snapshot. "That's me right there in the picture, right next to Him. See, I'm His dear child, an heir to the almighty God's eternal throne. He's my friend, my brother, my Savior. Yes, I once was the lost sheep. He left the whole flock to find me and bring me back home. Today, He called me by my new name. 'You are Branch,' He said. 'I'd know you anywhere. I AM your Vine.'"

Though it would seem this new identity thing is all about me, this text actually begins with Jesus reminding us of who He is.[7] It was no accident that He began His introduction to the new you with the words "I am." If He is I AM, He is the Giver of life. He nurtures us and sustains our lives with hope. He—I AM—is the living Word that called the stars into heaven's vaulted sky. He established light and crafted the elements of time, space, and change for His creation project. I AM feeds me with spiritual nutrients and life-giving water to keep my faith in Him alive. Conversely, if I were ever to become separated from Him, I could do nothing about it. Without Him, I perish.

There's more to this Vine and Branch relationship than merely being. This relationship gives a vested purpose to our identity.[8] The harvest His branches produce is heavy with sweet fruit pulp. This was the eternal Vintner's objective all along—a harvest that would yield the finest vintage of all time. Lift a glass! Offer a toast! The fruit from our well-nurtured vines has broken the world record for volume and excellence. It could only have happened because we are connected to Him. It is right that He should receive all the glory for such remarkable results. "Oh, taste and see that the LORD is good!" (Psalm 34:8).

---

6 See John 14:8–11.

7 Paul provided a clear summary of Christ's identity in Colossians 1:15–22.

8 Joel D. Biermann, *A Case for Character: Towards a Lutheran Virtue Ethics* (Minneapolis: Fortress, 2014), 177. Biermann writes, "Ethics matters to God because God has a will for creation. God's will for humanity is that each person be fully human—in possession of virtues which make one an able servant to the rest of creation. This is not a pursuit of virtue for the sake of virtue, but for the sake of conformity to Christ who is the perfect standard of what it means to be human."

CHIPPED, CRACKED, AND FRAGILE

Paul first identified himself, and then us, as clay jars. He wrote, "We have this treasure in jars of clay, to show that the surpassing power belongs to God and not to us. We are afflicted in every way, but not crushed; perplexed, but not driven to despair; persecuted, but not forsaken; struck down, but not destroyed" (2 Corinthians 4:7–9).

Have you ever thought of yourself as a clay jar? Precious oils, perfumes, high-end wines, fancy soaps, and costly liqueurs are often packaged in containers that distinguish the product as upscale. According to Paul, we are not fancy jars. By his description, we are just ordinary, clunky ceramic jugs and pots. God certainly could have done much better in choosing a more attractive container for carrying His precious grace to the lost, the last, the least, and the little.

Actually, being a container that is somewhat shabby in appearance is only half the problem. Have you looked in the mirror of God's Law lately? We are all cracked and chipped—vessels broken from the wear and tear of being a sinner. That's not what our loving Potter intended; it is what sin has done to us. Who knows where we've been kept or what unholy contents have been stored in us. Paul says,

> Not many of you were wise according to worldly standards, not many were powerful, not many were of noble birth. But God chose what is foolish in the world to shame the wise; God chose what is weak in the world to shame the strong; God chose what is low and despised in the world, even things that are not, to bring to nothing things that are, so that no human being might boast in the presence of God. And because of Him you are in Christ Jesus, who became to us wisdom from God, righteousness and sanctification and redemption, so that, as it is written, "Let the one who boasts, boast in the Lord." (1 Corinthians 1:26–31)

Sounds rude, but Paul was just being honest. "Such were some of you." Thankfully, Paul could add, "But you were washed, you were sanctified, you were justified in the name of the Lord Jesus Christ and by the Spirit of our God" (1 Corinthians 6:11).

Your new clay-pot identity is a part of your miracle transformation. Oh, how you have changed!

When God declared us "Not Guilty," He immediately called us back into His service without skipping a beat.[9] He wanted to put us to work in His great harvest, doing the tasks He had planned for us long before we were born, long be-

9 See John 21:15–17.

Filled with new life and a heart that is now beating in rhythm with His divine will, God has reissued the task of taking care of His creation.

fore the earth was born. Because we have been washed clean in Jesus' blood, we are once again of real value to God. Filled with new life and a heart that is now beating in rhythm with His divine will, God has reissued the task of taking care of His creation. There's plenty of work to be done. It is honorable work because we are serving the Lord and His people.

During the wilderness wanderings, that massive, colorful tent at the center of the Israelites' camp—the tabernacle—was the heart of their worship life. If we were to have visited the camp when sacrifices were being offered on God's altar, we would have been surprised by the bloody mess that offering sacrificial animals can be. It's likely that many twenty-first-century tourists would be sickened by the sights and smells. If we were assigned to cleanup duty, we would also be overwhelmed by the number of containers needed to keep the area clean. These ceramic mugs, jugs, pots, jars, and bowls had been donated by local potters. However, before they could be used, every one of them had to be ceremonially cleansed and officially declared "clean." This little ritual also meant that these clay pots were henceforth dedicated for tabernacle use only. Once they had been properly consecrated, the pots could never again be used in a commercial or domestic capacity. They literally belonged to God and henceforth could be used only in His service.

You and I are similarly consecrated for God's service. It is an honor and a privilege to serve the Maker of heaven and earth, even as a humble pot.[10] What an awesome responsibility it is to carry His life-giving water to anyone thirsting for some good news! But the apostle is quick to remind us that "the surpassing power belongs to God and not to us" (2 Corinthians 4:7). God uses us for transporting His precious Gospel. The power to change hearts is His. He is God; we are not.

Being a ceramic pot can be hazardous. When filled with liquid, kiln-fired jars are actually quite fragile. Handlers are not always careful about banging them against one another when moving them or storing them. We will have to endure many pressures in this life because of our faith in Jesus. Considering the precious contents that God has entrusted to our care and keeping, the apostle assures us we will endure. As God's ragtag collection of broken, shattered, chipped, and cracked ceramic pots, we are virtually indestructible.

10 See 1 Peter 2:5–9; Ezekiel 11:19; 36:26–27.

AGENTS OF CHANGE

When Jesus preached His famous Sermon on the Mount, He was direct in giving His followers another new identity, saying, "You are the salt of the earth" (Matthew 5:13). Like the other identities that God has marked us with, our identity as metaphorical salt flows from our identity in Christ Jesus. We are salty because He is salty. And as salt, we are again useful in His kingdom's work. In fact, as salt, we are agents of change, here to make a difference in the lives of the people around us. In this respect, we are like Jesus, the heavenly Father's great agent for changing our spiritually shattered relationship with Him.

We are salty because He is salty. And as salt, we are again useful in His kingdom's work.

Salt causes change. It heals wounds, melts ice, adds flavor to food, preserves meat, sanitizes surfaces, and cauterizes wounds. When Christians walk into a room filled with people, everything changes. We are the salt of the earth. Your saltiness, and mine, rubs off on our surroundings and the people in them. We alter their culture just by being. Whether you address a crowd or talk to a child, something is happening to them, or perhaps even in them. They are influenced by your demeanor, your warmth, your smile, your extended hand. Being in your presence places them into Christ's presence. They experience the kindness that Jesus embodied in His life. They see that God's people conduct their business with integrity. Your life is a sermon that preaches the Christian faith and biblical truth. You invite their respect with the twinkle in your eye. They see the joy you have in knowing that you are a member of God's family.

In the open hostility of today's secular culture, we stand out. Our godly behavior distinguishes us as unique. Our love for others sets us apart from the godless lovelessness of unbelief. We make a difference. We especially make a difference for people who are difficult to love.

Unbelievers can be difficult to love. They hate what Christianity represents.[11] They hate Jesus. They are offended by the Gospel. They resist the Spirit's efforts to reach out to them with God's grace. Our sinful nature tempts us to hate them in return. Godly love moves us to follow the example Jesus gave us when He prayed that His Father would forgive His executioners. But loving one's enemy is not an easy thing to do. Ken Cherney explains:

> The Christian life is not lived out in heaven, where the risen Christ is enthroned at his Father's side, surrounded by ranks of angels and bathed in unapproachable light. Our life is lived out here on earth,

11 See John 17:14.

We are the hope-filled light of a future reality with Jesus that is so desperately needed in a culture that has disowned God.

> where Christ was crucified. . . . Often, however, its essence [the Christian's cross] is the hostile and indifferent reception that the Christian's deeds of love meet with out in the world. Christian love is utterly defenseless as it makes its way through this godless world. Love must be prepared to be misunderstood, rejected, taken advantage of, and abused. . . . At these moments the resemblance of the Christian's cross to that of his Lord becomes clear.[12]

Jesus had barely finished introducing God's people to their new identity as the salt of the earth when He added yet another feature of our new Christian identity.

> You are the light of the world. A city set on a hill cannot be hidden. Nor do people light a lamp and put it under a basket, but on a stand, and it gives light to all in the house. In the same way, let your light shine before others, so that they may see your good works and give glory to your Father who is in heaven. (Matthew 5:14–16)

In contrast to the humbling identities Jesus gave to us as the salt of the earth and pots of clay, being light makes star performers of us. As beacons of light for a world stumbling around in the dark, you and I provide a prophetic glimpse of what the new reality of God's heavenly kingdom will be like in eternal glory. There, we will shine for Jesus. On earth, we are the light for all who still imagine there's no heaven, no transcendent kingdom of God, no moral right and wrong, no Creator, no sin, no miracle interventions, no glimpse of Jesus' glory light shining in their lives. We are the hope-filled light of a future reality with Jesus that is so desperately needed in a culture that has disowned God. We reflect His light,[13] making a difference for people who need Jesus to light their way to life everlasting.

A believer's reflected light does more than merely change the circumstances of miserable lives; it changes the direction in which people's lives are headed. Illuminating the entire countryside from a hilltop, Christ's saving light calls sinners to come and find protection and peace in the city of God. "Go therefore and make disciples of all nations, baptizing them in the name of the Father and of the Son

12 Ken Cherney, "Hidden in Plain Sight: Luther's Doctrine of Vocation," *Wisconsin Lutheran Quarterly* 98, no. 4 (2001): 283. Used with permission.

13 Cherney, "Hidden," 284. "Through my vocation, I take my place between God and my neighbor and become a conduit through which divine blessings reach others. In Luther's terminology, I become 'the mask' God wears or 'the hands' God uses as he does his work in the world."

and of the Holy Spirit, teaching them to observe all that I have commanded you" (Matthew 28:19–20a).

THE GREAT MAKEOVER

If there is such a thing as a biblical rationale for living the godly life, this is it. God has laid out our existential reason for being. You and I have been given the same purpose for which God created the human race—to proclaim His glorious and eternal presence to the created universe. Our Creator honors us with the privilege of participating in His great renovation project of returning His kingdom to its original splendor. This is why Christian character rises above common character. In the words of Biermann:

God has laid out our existential reason for being.

> To pursue virtue is to pursue the restoration of God's creation, the very reason for God's work of justifying fallen humans. Christians strive to grow in virtues and the consequent production of good works for their fellow creatures simply because this is their appropriate work as redeemed creatures—it is what they have been put here to do. . . . Christians strive for virtue not to perfect their nature or to achieve personal fulfillment, still less to win divine favor. They seek to gain a character stamped with virtue because they are acutely aware that this is the standard that Christ himself has established for humanity.[14]

14 Joel Biermann, *Character*, 156, 176.

I am reminded of your sincere faith, a faith that dwelt first in your grandmother Lois and your mother Eunice and now, I am sure, dwells in you as well. For this reason I remind you to fan into flame the gift of God, which is in you through the laying on of my hands.

—2 Timothy 1:5–6

CHAPTER 11

A Moral Education

Between ages 4 and 17, American children spend about one-sixth of their time getting a good education. All of it, at least indirectly, has ethical implications. Regardless of whether it happens in a public school, a private school, or a parochial school, learning has a major impact on what our nation's children know and believe. For better or worse, schools are shaping the next generation of young Americans, both in terms of each child's identity and his or her lifelong performance. The long and short of it is that education plays a major role in shaping the character of future generations.

The long and short of it is that education plays a major role in shaping the character of future generations.

MORAL EDUCATION IN COLONIAL AMERICA

When the first immigrants came to the shores of North America, they brought their ideas about moral education with them. Learning typically took place in the home. Content had strong ethical overtones. Most of the moral educational content was rooted in the soil of Protestantism—including the particular ilk of Protestantism known as Arminianism.[1]

1 Roland Cap Ehlke, *Like a Pelting Rain: The Making of the Modern Mind,* abridged version (Milwaukee: EhlkeWorks, 2013), 21. Ehlke writes, "Arminianism came to represent such tendencies as liberalism, the propensity to attribute some sort of innate goodness to human nature, an emphasis on man's free will, an inclination toward an intellectualized interpretation of Scripture, and a leaning toward Rome. . . . Arminianism especially protested against dogmas that conflicted with reason."

Two seventeenth-century literary giants helped establish an ethical groundwork. The first was the English poet and polemicist John Milton (1608–74). Milton, the author of *Paradise Lost*, "regarded biblical revelation as the source of true knowledge."[2] John Bunyan (1628–88), Milton's contemporary, expressed his unwavering faith in the classic work *The Pilgrim's Progress,* an allegory so "steeped in the Bible and Christian teaching [that] . . . conversations seem to have been lifted straight from a catechism. Everything, including nature, attests to Scripture's teachings."[3] Both men wrote their great works at a time in English history of intense social and religious upheaval. Both looked to the past, retaining a respect for Scripture and its Gospel teachings centered in Christ and His cross.[4]

Life in the colonies tended to revolve around rigid religious ideals and separatist worldviews. Yet, there were indications that the colonial foundation of a culture steeped in a biblical worldview was about to discover two new concepts that would change the collective worldviews of the young colonies. The first was known as religious tolerance.[5] The second became known as the separation of church and state. In time, these two radical ideas would change the face of moral education in America in ways that would essentially remove the biblical ethic from the national agenda, replacing it with an ethic rooted in secular values and humanistic principles. By the middle of the eighteenth century, a more pragmatic worldview was already generating pressure to move moral education in the same direction that the culture was leaning. The culture was noticeably leaning in the direction of galvanizing support for alternative concepts such as equality, freedom, tolerance, and democracy.

NEW PRESUPPOSITIONS

By the end of the eighteenth century, science and the scientific method, which was then thought to be a foolproof way of ascertaining truth in nature, was challenging biblical truth and Reformation values.[6] Known as the Age of Enlightenment, "much of eighteenth-century thought was centered on using reason in all areas of life. Inspired by Isaac Newton, other thinkers began looking for laws to

---

2 Ehlke, *Pelting Rain*, 26.

3 Ehlke, *Pelting Rain*, 27.

4 Ehlke, *Pelting Rain*, 28. Ehlke writes, "Milton and Bunyan retained the old respect for Scripture. And while both stood in opposition to the establishment, they did not stand in opposition to basic Christian theology, including the central tenet of redemption through Christ."

5 Religious tolerance emerged as a new concept in late-seventeenth-century England, during the tumultuous years when sectarian groups vied for control of the political center. John Locke (1632–1704) laid the philosophical groundwork for religious tolerance in a writing entitled "A Letter Concerning Tolerance" (1689). This document would later become known as his social contract theory. A century later, Locke's letter influenced the writings of Voltaire and Rousseau.

6 Expressed in the writings of Alexander Pope (1688–1744) and Voltaire (1694–1778), the new interest in science gave rise to a sectarian school of thought known as English Deism.

explain not simply the physical world but other aspects of human life and experience as well."[7]

As Reformation values shaped the culture, Western Europe became a fertile ground for emerging new sectarian groups. Each group struggled to define its position by writing carefully worded doctrinal statements. A counter-reformation mitigated for a worldview "less dogmatic, less passionate, more reasonable, and more tolerant. In the process, the more extreme representatives of this group began to develop a new worldview known as deism."[8] Glenn Sunshine explains what distinguishes deism from biblical Christianity.

> In historic Christianity, God's nature can be described in part by three pairs of terms:
>
> **God is infinite**—He transcends space, time, and number—while at the same time he is personal. As a Trinity, he is relational by nature and therefore can have relationships with people.
>
> **God is the Creator of the universe and also its sustainer.** Its continuing existence and operation depend on His supporting activity.
>
> **God is transcendent**—He is utterly beyond the universe and anything the human mind can conceive—yet He is also immanent, that is, immediately present with us at all times.
>
> Deists generally accepted the first terms in each of these pairs while rejecting the second. In other words, God is infinite but not personal; He is the Creator, but the universe operates on its own without any involvement by God; and He is transcendent but not immanent.[9]

Deists used the metaphor of a great clockmaker to describe God and His work.[10] Their logic argued that if we accept God as perfect, all-powerful, and transcendent, it would be impossible for Him to create a universe that required His constant intervention. Thus, a deist's worldview denounced divine miracles and Jesus' work as Redeemer, both acts of divine intervention. Sunshine calls deism an "unstable worldview" because God's only role "is to kick-start the universe."[11]

7 Sunshine, *Why You Think*, 140.

8 Sunshine, *Why You Think*, 136.

9 Sunshine, *Why You Think*, 136–37.

10 Deists were already on very thin ice with a starting point that assumed God is like humans.

11 Sunshine, *Why You Think*, 163–64. Sunshine adds, "If another alternative can be found to explain how the universe got here, we can safely eliminate God from the system altogether. All that is needed is a plausible-sounding explanation for the universe, and we are left with a world consisting only of matter and energy—a metaphysical system known as naturalism or materialism."

In other words, God is God; nature is not.

Deism is important to our conversation because it is the key to understanding the historical process that would eventually lay the groundwork for Darwin and his ideas about the origin of humankind.[12]

Today, a wide range of disparate worldviews represent the science community's understanding of cause. While general science has effectively removed God from its underlying presuppositions, the range leaves room on one end of the spectrum for those who see God's hand in every aspect of nature to the opposite extreme of those who maintain that all interactions of matter and energy are rooted in natural processes and order (materialism). For those who read Scripture as inspired revelation, the psalmist narrowed the field to a single cause, writing: "The heavens declare the glory of God, and the sky above proclaims His handiwork" (Psalm 19:1). In other words, God is God; nature is not.

COMMON SCHOOLS

As populations became more ethnically diverse in the Northeast, the idea of a common school to Americanize local immigrants became popular. Since religion and education were generally construed as serving the same social purpose, Protestant churches along the Atlantic seaboard often organized the local public school's curriculum. For example, the *McGuffey Reader*, ostensibly designed to teach reading, also became the purveyor of Calvinist doctrine. The little reader featured heavy doses of moralizing principles.[13]

In one sense, common schools provided a good base for rethinking the Old World social order that inevitably revolved around a culture's religious identity. For its governing apparatus to work, American society needed to bring the disparate religious groups together in a posture of common support and goodwill aimed at attaining the greater social good. In a pluralistic society, such a governing apparatus could not be a support system rooted in specific religious convictions.

12 Sunshine, *Why You Think*, 166–68. Sunshine exposes Darwinism for what it is, writing, "For people who found naturalism appealing, Darwin's theory was a godsend. It was the missing link needed to round out a fully naturalistic worldview. . . . [But] for a theory to be scientific, it must be able to be validated through the scientific method: A theory is proposed and predictions are made from it. These predictions are then tested through experimentation. . . . Darwinism is not itself subject to the scientific method any more than anything in history is. The past is over; you cannot revisit it, observe it, test it, or experiment on it. All you can do is look at the surviving evidence and try to make sense of it. . . . But, of course, none of this matters because Darwinism is not a scientific theory but a worldview assumption, and as such, it is not falsifiable. . . . No matter how many failed predictions come from Darwinism, it can never be proven false. Simply put, naturalistic evolution is an article of faith."

13 Moralizing is the practice of preaching about right and wrong from a position of moral superiority. (See Matthew 7:1.)

THE GERMAN-LUTHERAN WAVE

In the mid-1800s, German-Lutheran immigrants began to settle in the rich farming territories of the Midwest. Groups of German-Lutheran congregations formed federations known as synods. Like Luther, these Lutherans believed that moral training, rooted in Scripture, should begin in the home. They also agreed with Luther that a more formal style of training should be continued in school, when children were old enough. Part of their rationale was aimed at maintaining flavors of the culture they were used to in their homeland. Moreover, the practical Germans had a cultural bias that favored efficiency. When the community's children were in school, the rest of the family was free to pursue their work of maintaining the family farm. A deeper concern, however, focused on defending and protecting Lutheran theological positions. Bible stories and training in Luther's Small Catechism were the hallmarks of the German-Lutheran curriculum. To sustain an educational model that was primarily dedicated to teaching God's Word from the Lutheran perspectives of Scripture alone, faith alone, and grace alone, German Lutherans made a firm commitment to own and operate their own Lutheran schools.

Bible stories and training in Luther's Small Catechism were the hallmarks of the German-Lutheran curriculum.

German-Lutheran schools were usually attached to local congregations or associations of congregations. The children of nonmembers were generally welcomed, but space for them was often limited. Tuition was modest, and the cost of running Lutheran parochial schools was typically absorbed by the sponsoring congregation(s). The Lutheran Church—Missouri Synod (LCMS), the Wisconsin Evangelical Lutheran Synod (WELS), and the Evangelical Lutheran Synod (ELS, a Norwegian group) recognized the need for maintaining control over local classroom theology.[14] Each of these synods organized (and continue to operate) teacher training schools to provide a steady stream of teachers formally trained in Lutheran theology.

14 In 1872, these three Lutheran synods formed the Evangelical Lutheran Synodical Conference of North America. Their unifying statements of belief were the Lutheran Confessions. The synodical conference was disbanded in 1967 due to doctrinal differences. Today, all three continue to serve God's people with strong, parochial early childhood programs, elementary schools, high schools, and colleges.

PURGING THE BIBLICAL ETHIC

In the waning decades of the nineteenth century, many local public schools became part of school systems. These systems (eventually structured as school districts) could be more aggressive in seeking public funding. Taxpayers were now required to support the public schools in their district. Most of those schools were essentially promoting sectarian dogma. It wasn't long before taxpayers demanded a change in the moral content of the schools they were funding.

Under the leadership of education reformer Horace Mann (1796–1859), a movement to eliminate tools such as the *McGuffey Reader* began dismantling sectarian influence in tax-funded public schools. To a greater degree, this was accomplished without disturbing the traditional moral core of the curriculum. The Ten Commandments, for example, were taught as they had always been taught. But, if the Gospel of salvation in Christ Jesus had once been part and parcel of the moral content of a public-school education (though in many places this is to be doubted), any Gospel emphasis was now quietly dismissed. For many, including many members of the community who did not claim Christian orientation, the moral behaviors that the Ten Commandments emphasized were still necessary for maintaining social order.

Shortly after the end of World War I (1914–18), an educational theorist named John Dewey (1859–1952) began to push for a new moral foundation for secular education that would be free from all religious influence. Under Dewey's influence, moral authority shifted away from biblical truth. Dewey's educational philosophy favored this notion:

> Children were to be regarded as having the capacity to determine their own moral standards. He believed that the natural tendency toward justice and goodness resided within the intellectual and moral faculties of the child. Dewey and his colleagues agreed that the definition of moral behavior depended more upon the circumstances in which the individual existed than upon a code of a priori rules.[15]

The changes John Dewey and his colleagues introduced failed to provide substantive answers to questions about right and wrong. The moral heart of public education in America slid deeper into the abyss of humanistic principles.[16] And now, this twisted worldview also lacked a clear understanding of any particular moral authority or its application in the lives of children. Over the next four de-

15 Hunter, *Death*, 60–61.

16 Hunter, *Death*, 61. He writes, "Morality, for Dewey, originated in society; all ethical and moral understanding, therefore, was social. Identity too was social."

cades, a mix of communal norms, biblical virtues, social clichés, and traditional mores filled the vacuum.

PSYCHOLOGICAL HUMANISM

Meanwhile, another major shift toward a new ethic was gaining attention in academia. Until late in the nineteenth century, psychology was studied as a part of philosophical thought and was broadly defined as the study of the mind. Today, psychology is both an academic query and an applied discipline that endeavors to understand human behaviors (and their pathologies), functions of the brain, personality traits and characteristics, attitudes, learning and cognition, imaginative thought, and so on. For our conversation, it must be noted that psychology has increasingly exerted its influence over the last 150 years on how the contemporary mind approaches morality. In his book *The Death of Character: Moral Education in an Age without Good or Evil* (pp. 177–92), James Hunter explains how John Dewey, for example, introduced an approach to secular moral education that was rooted in a nonbiblical understanding of right and wrong, and which drew its credence from a witch's blend of deistic philosophy and the new science of psychology. Hunter calls this concept psychological humanism because it is partly rooted in the legitimate science of psychology and partly rooted in humanistic ethics. Thinkers such as Erik Erikson, Benjamin Spock, Carl Rogers, B. F. Skinner, and Rudolf Dreikurs were in the vanguard, insinuating psychology into the question "What constitutes the moral life?" Secular educational models used the opportunity to effectively remove any remaining remnants of the biblical ethic. Students were encouraged to develop their own values, based on experience and natural instinct.

This unbiblical approach to living the moral life continues to haunt American education today. Some Christian schools are also inclined to combine God's objective Law with every student's subjective interpretation. This approach essentially creates an ethic that subsumes the whole notion of placing humankind in the judgment seat, while the almighty and eternal God occupies the dock.

UNDERLYING CAUSES

So, why did American education abandon its biblical moral foundation in favor of human philosophies that directly oppose Scripture? James Hunter identifies three basic causes.

Parents need to have a practical understanding of the moral content their children are being taught.

1. Culture shapes educational models and content (not the reverse).[17]

Most of us believe that education transforms the masses. This is a myth. Hunter writes, "Moral education has always been more about conformity than about transformation. The question we face is, of course, conformity to what?"[18]

Hunter's question has been the central issue in moral education in America for a very long time. When he asks, "Conformity to what?" he is really inviting us to consider who defines moral behavior. In a pluralistic society, an answer from virtually any quarter will immediately impact the way the rest of us treat one another.

When the children of Israel wandered the Sinai Peninsula, God established the civil law, the ceremonial law, and the moral law. He also enforced it, guided the culture, and drove the media. The Israelites were bound to God and one another in a common worldview that was unambiguously theocratic.

America has never imagined itself as a theocratic nation, not even when Christian voices represented a majority. Nor are we suggesting that our country should pursue such a course now. That would be as foolish as imagining a world without God. The tendency throughout most of American history has been a constant tug in the opposite direction, toward openness, tolerance, diversity, and without any sectarian interference in the moral way that people choose to live. The terminal point for such a ludicrous position is a moral vacuum, leaving people to try to answer the tough questions about right and wrong by dipping into a deep and empty bucket. This is a serious problem because we are speaking about concepts that define our humanness—truth, faith, integrity, justice.

These kinds of questions arise daily in the microcultures of American classrooms. They are the why questions every two-year-old depends on to gain real and lasting insights into life's inherent dangers and pitfalls. It is virtually impossible to teach any secular subject without bumping into ethical questions. It is equally difficult to maintain discipline or develop an appropriate social decorum without referencing moral character, right behaviors, or the authority that will hold us accountable to some kind of social standards.

17 Hunter, *Death*, 27. Hunter writes, "As much as we want to think of moral education as having potential to shape society, the stronger direction of influence is the way in which society shapes, even dictates, the content of education."

18 Hunter, *Death*, 27.

The whole discussion of ethics in American schools has been generally met with a deafening silence, or at the very least, an uneasy indifference. Parents need to have a practical understanding of the moral content their children are being taught. They need to know what the moral assumptions of their child's school are—where they originated and what kind of outcomes they are aimed at producing. This is their right, and not merely a privilege. Sadly, such vital information has been cordoned off and placed on reserve, only to be shared with parents on a "need to know" basis.

2. Cultures do not last forever.[19]

Cultural change occurs at such a slow pace that it happens largely undetected. Hunter uses the scholarly term "habitus" to describe how repeated lessons and reiterated traditions create a habitual way of thinking.[20] "Habitus," says Hunter, "refers to the taken-for-granted assumptions that prevail in a particular society or civilization that make our experience of the world seem commonsensical."[21] He explains that major philosophical issues are inevitable when habitus is no longer able to keep pace with a culture that is racing ahead.

The rapid cultural changes that occurred after 1970 forced the corresponding shift in moral education to accelerate. When people began to see their national habitus disintegrating, they became insecure about their well-established anchors for living the moral life. Hunter says that when habitus wears thin, we are forced to ask core-level questions we have never before had to confront—questions such as these:

> What, after all, is a family? What are "family values"? How do we ideally raise children? What do we tell them about meaning in life? Where is it found? How [do we] attain it? And what do we tell them of the rules for living an honorable life? To whom or what do they appeal when seeking direction in their lives? The confusion over these rather basic issues spills out into public controversies over gender, sexuality, the family; over the nature of art, faith, and life

---

19 Hunter, *Death*, 223. Hunter writes, "Though we all imagine that the culture we live in is stable and dependable, there are also good reasons to believe that we underestimate the degree to which there has been a dissolution in the system of dispositions that give common meaning to our moral vocabulary and coherence and purpose to our moral aspirations. How so? American culture has always been in flux."

20 Biermann, *Character*, 110. "Why do parents worry about where their children go to school, about their playmates and peers, about the ways they use their free time, about the television shows they watch? They worry because all of us know that Aristotle was—at least to some extent—right. Moral virtue *is* habit long continued. The inner spirit is shaped and developed by the structures within which we live, the things we see and do daily."

21 Hunter, *Death*, 222.

> itself; over the meaning of justice, public welfare, tolerance, and liberty; over the purpose of schools, philanthropy, technology, and markets.[22]

3. Character flows from convictions.[23]

Hunter does not make this point from the worldview of a Christian. He is referring to character in a generic sense. But, since our conversation centers on the tension between secular character and Christian character, we prefer to make the point that, while secular character and Christian character may, in some instances, appear to be quite similar, they are distinguishable by the object of one's faith.

The object of a Christian's faith is God's faithfulness to His unchanging promises.

The object of a Christian's faith is God's faithfulness to His unchanging promises. God's people must talk about what happens when the culture we are living in destroys our "creeds, convictions, and the 'god-terms' that made those creeds sacred to us and inviolable within us."[24] How will the destruction of our sacred truths, the dismissal of God's authoritative presence, or the demolition of our sacred creeds impact our lives or threaten the faith of future generations? And how will we respond?

Someone will be quick to point out that God will protect His church from extinction. Nevertheless, the challenges we face are formidable. At the very least, we will want to become better informed about the spiritual landscape we inhabit.

A STATUS REPORT ON MORAL EDUCATION IN AMERICA

In our era, the moral foundations of America's public schools have been thoroughly secularized. Many of us still need to come to grips with this fact. Moreover, the rift that separates secular education from Christian education deepens. This gulf is growing partly because of the philosophical differences between bib-

22 Hunter, *Death*, 223.

23 Hunter, *Death*, xiii. Hunter writes, "Character is formed in relation to convictions and is manifested in the capacity to abide by those convictions even in, *especially in*, the face of temptation. This being so, the demise of character begins with the destruction of creeds, the convictions, and the 'god-terms' that made those creeds sacred to us and inviolable within us."

24 Hunter, *Death*, 17. Hunter argues, "The sacred quality of these moral imperatives cannot be overstated. Character is formed through the slow reception of 'god-terms' deep within us—god-terms, as Philip Rieff put it, that exist as 'presiding presences.' As such, character is shaped not by a cowering acquiescence to rules imposed externally but as conscious, directed obedience to truths authoritatively received and affirmed. In this way the imperatives of social life—both positive in obligation or negative in prohibition and repression—possess a moral power that we recognize as transcending ourselves. By virtue of the authority invested in it, morality is inwardly compelling; it exerts a leverage upon our will. When it speaks to us, we conform to it."

lical ethics and cultural mores. More often, it is because both educational models are vying for the same students. In some cases, they are also vying for the same dollars.[25] This means it is incumbent on us to know what distinguishes the secular educational model from the Christian model.[26]

To begin, the worldview taught in secular schools does not acknowledge either God or His transcendent kingdom. Lutheran theologian Lyle Lange writes:

> Parents who send their children to public schools need to remember, however, that it is not the state's concern to meet the spiritual needs of their children. It is the parents' responsibility at home to meet the spiritual needs of their children (Eph 6:4). The church will be able to help parents in the spiritual training of their children, but only in a limited way. Confirmation class, Sunday school or teen Bible class, youth group, and regular worship will be of value, but parents have to remember that their children are daily facing assaults on their faith in public schools. Public education is not "religionless" education. The religion of public education is the religion of the Old Adam—work righteousness. Its philosophy is contrary to Scripture. People are portrayed as basically good. Nothing is considered a sin. . . . Guilt is said to ruin a good self-image.[27]

The law that prohibits the teaching of a biblical understanding of God's Word in a public forum is binding. Children attending secular schools are enveloped in a curriculum and climate that embraces a worldview that is essentially limited to life in the here and now.[28] Yet, this same curriculum promotes the teaching of some moral and religious views that are essentially anti-biblical, anti–two kingdoms, and ultimately anti-Christ. Unless parents make a concerted effort to counter such false views by keeping Jesus and His cross at the center of their family's daily life, even those children who are raised in Christian households will de-

---

25 The competition for students is fierce. Over the last half century, Christian school systems have expanded their markets to include the entire community. Many of these schools approached this decision as direct response to Jesus' Great Commission (Matthew 28:19–20). But the shift, at least in part, was also a response to a concern about declining enrollments. In those states where a voucher system gives a variety of school choices to low-income families, private schools have also increased in number, forcing both public schools and parochial schools to recruit students from the same community to maintain their level of financial support from the state.

26 See *Appendix C: Two Different Worldviews.*

27 Lange, *God So Loved*, 647–48.

28 Hunter, *Death*, 24. Hunter writes, "The moral culture, in other words, is not merely the environment within which identity plays out. It is, even more, a reality that frames the categories of identity, structures the identity, and even indelibly stamps identity. Without the authoritative presence of moral culture, internalized into subjective consciousness, there can be no character or 'character development.'"

God's Law will never change.

velop a worldview that assumes a one-kingdom understanding of their life's reality.

Secular models essentially ignore God's existence altogether. This effectively eliminates any practical need for the First, Second, and Third Commandments. In the secular worldview, Commandments 4–10, which once held some torque in American society, have been deemed outmoded by humanistic views about social issues such as gender, sexuality, marriage, abortion, and euthanasia. Even the most common definitions of honesty, or respect for the property of others, have shifted rather dramatically. This so-called "new morality" flies in the face of Scripture and God's moral code. Moreover, secular worldviews are constantly in the state of flux. They have, therefore, become a destabilizing cause for social anxiety, confusion, and civil disruption. Conversely, God's Law will never change. In fact, the Lord has issued dire warnings about changing His Law in even the slightest detail.[29]

The secular educational model does not teach, or even acknowledge, that Jesus is every child's Savior from sin. A secular ethic does not teach children to forgive one another in Jesus' name, bless one another with Jesus' love, recognize one another's unique talents as gifts from God, or strive to do their very best as a way of glorifying God's name. Christian schools make it their primary mission to build their curriculum and culture around the Bible's Good News that Jesus came to earth to rescue mankind from the curse of sin.

In secular schools, personal identity is frequently confused with performance. High achievement is usually promoted as the greatest objective for students. It is emphasized even before children have a firm understanding of their own identity. Since God's kingdom is not recognized, the secular objective of high achievement is necessarily limited to preparing students for life in earthly kingdoms. At the same time, a secular curriculum trains children to find their fullest satisfaction in life by seeking glory for their own efforts. Training in self-glorification embeds narcissism in a child's habitus. It acts like a psychological drug. It is almost impossible to give it up because the hearts and minds of children who have learned to think this way inevitably assume there is nothing more to life than one's performance.

Christian schools also stress high achievement. But in the ethic of a biblical learning environment, life's purpose is not understood as self-serving or self-promoting, nor is it intended to earn God's favor. Instead, children attending Christian schools learn to appreciate their talents and abilities as gifts from God. They learn that working hard to achieve a level of excellence and using the gifts God

29 See Revelation 22:18–19.

has given them is done to the glory of God's name.

On the whole, schools that are rooted in Scripture begin to address personal identity from a biblical perspective at a very early age.

On the whole, schools that are rooted in Scripture begin to address personal identity from a biblical perspective at a very early age. And they continue to nurture godly identity throughout the child's formal training. Additionally, in Bible-based schools, students are fed daily with the saving message that they are God's children, loved by God, and forgiven for Jesus' sake. The teachers in Christian schools teach from a biblical worldview because they understand how important Jesus is in their own lives. They know that God has promised to bless their faith in Jesus with hope in a real, enchanted future with Him in heaven.

All this said, there are many geographic locations and family situations that limit the educational choices parents have. Throughout Scripture, God repeatedly instructs Christian parents to personally nurture the spiritual formation of their children. This is the most important part of God's mandate to Christian parents. No school setting, no educational model—parochial, private, or secular—can ever become a substitute for parental guidance and modeling. And this is true at all levels of education during a child's growing years. When parents fail to create a home environment in which God's Word is read regularly, when they fail to position Jesus Christ and His cross at the center of their family's spiritual lives, when they neglect to teach their children that godly love leads family members to live in harmony, patience, and forgiveness, when they do not provide living examples to train their children to understand that morality is a response to God's grace, children will be confused about their faith, and they will continually be challenged by a weak or false understanding of who they are and what their purpose in life is.

Like Adam and Eve, we lack the spiritual wisdom of God to know what is good for us and our children. In the context of our discussion about schools, it is vital for God's people to understand the dilemma we face. We need to know what getting "a good education" really means.[30] Carl Lawrenz and John Jeske have written about this dilemma in very direct language. What they have said should echo in

30 Gregory A. Boyd, *The Myth of a Christian Nation: How the Quest for Political Power Is Destroying the Church* (Grand Rapids: Zondervan, 2005), 27. Boyd writes, "Followers of Jesus must realize—and must help others realize—that the hope of the world lies not in any particular version of the kingdom of the world gaining the upper hand in Babylon's endless tit-for-tat game. The hope of the world lies in a kingdom that is not of this world, a kingdom that doesn't participate in tit for tat, a kingdom that operates with a completely different understanding of power. It is the kingdom established by Jesus Christ and a kingdom that is expanded by people committed to following him. It is the kingdom of God."

our ears every time we wrestle with the question of raising godly children in a godless culture.

> Sinful man tenaciously clings to the thought that paradisaic bliss and glory may after all be attainable in this life. . . . Man constantly deceives himself into thinking that his malady is after all nothing more than a question of proper environment. Man hopes to reenter Paradise by creating a paradisaic environment for himself by finding better housing, better schooling, better recreation; by improving ecology, through distributing wealth, through prosperity, and through an abundance of material possessions; by making progress in banishing ignorance, poverty, and disease. . . . None of these things mentioned are, of course, wrong in themselves. . . . What is wrong, and at the same time vain and futile, is man's feverish effort and hope of again turning this earthly life into a paradise. What is wrong is when sinful man forgets that ever since the fall, the main function of this earthly life is to serve as a time of grace. . . . Man above all needs to take refuge in faith through God's saving grace that is held out to him as a free gift in the gospel message.[31]

31 Lawrenz and Jeske, *Genesis 1–11*, 169.

How then will they call on Him in whom they have not believed? And how are they to believe in Him of whom they have never heard? And how are they to hear without someone preaching? And how are they to preach unless they are sent? As it is written, "How beautiful are the feet of those who preach the good news!"

—Romans 10:14–15

CHAPTER 12

In the Media Torrent

Our ability to communicate across time and space and in an ever-changing environment is vital. Communication is the key to sharing our human experience. Relationships rise or fall on the strength of thoughts conveyed with intelligible grunts and groans, facial expressions, ink spots on parchment, dots on an illuminated screen, recorded messages, or colorful, neon-filled tubes. Words express our humanity. Language—written and spoken, read and heard—has the potential to explain to others who we are, how we feel, and what we know. Our ability to communicate is among the most powerful tools (or weapons) in the human toolbox.

Words express our humanity.

Deep-level communication is in our DNA. No other creature in Eden received this gift. Cows can't diagram their family tree. Elephants find it impossible to spin a sonnet or tell a lie. Pigs are useless when it comes to humming a tune from a musical score. A few species can be taught to respond to simple commands. Some even have the capacity to remember them, but they are unable to write a book that teaches their offspring the meaning of life. Only mankind engages in the arts, fine or applied. Only the human creature processes ideas from the past, develops them, and then passes them on in a new form to the next generation.

Poetry captures our imagination. It lifts us to the edge of our human experience, often leaving us with the alluring sense of having abandoned time, space, and change altogether. Song is poetry. Melody parallels vocal inflections in speech. The rhythms of music mimic the rhythms of life.

Prose, on the other hand, is rooted in the soil of logic and order. It engages our intellect with concepts that are tangible and definitive. The daily news is prose. The language of law is prose. Counting, measuring, or stating theorems are prosaic functions. So are algorithms.

Prose thrives on story. It appreciates time and has a healthy respect for history and facts. It tends to be linear. Most stories have a beginning, a middle, and an end. Stories recount the cause-and-effect events of life, often in a linear fashion that chronicles the beginning, middle, and end of a life cycle.

Like poetry, stories help shape our worldview. Some stories entertain. Some teach. Some model heroes or expose antiheroes. Some sound an alarm. Other stories encourage, define values, or set norms. Stories tell us who we are and who we are not. They tell us what is acceptable and what is not acceptable. Stories are intensely relational; therefore, they are also character driven.

A MOVING IMAGE

Shortly after World War II, a new storytelling medium emerged. Someone called it "television." The name stuck. The new medium reached out to the masses and quickly became the premier tool for communicating the stories that shaped our future.

Television features moving pictures over words. It appeals to our sense of vision, where image and movement play to the dominant sense of our species, which is sight.

As it turns out, the old saying "a picture is worth a thousand words" is more profound than anyone could have imagined. If one is looking for even more visual impact, one ups the ante by making the image move. A moving picture is worth many thousands of words. Given its power to engage us with moving images, television has the capacity to quickly bypass thought and capture the attention of our emotions long before our brains can kick into gear.

Television became available to the general public in the mid-1940s. By 1967, close enough to John Lennon's "Imagine" song to make the date noteworthy, Marshall McLuhan and Quentin Fiore published a pocket-sized book entitled *The Medium is the Massage*. The little book chronicled television's cultural impact during its brief twenty-five-year lifespan. One of the book's more pointed observations noted a significant change in the traditional parental role because of television's cultural influence.

> The family circle has widened. The worldpool of information fathered by electric media . . . far surpasses any possible influence

> mom and dad can now bring to bear. Character no longer is shaped by only two earnest, fumbling experts. Now all the world's a sage.[1]

That quotation was written a half century ago. Our culture is still living in the shadows of that observation. The impact television continues to have on the family has increased exponentially since 1967, while the number of new media offerings has grown. The influence that television had on family life was so profound that in 2002, Todd Gitlin could write, "Life experience has become an experience in the presence of media."[2] Gitlin's description of how people filled the void of lost, broken, or mind-numbingly tedious family relationships is still stunning in how accurately it describes many American homes even today:

> Like flesh-and-blood people, the ones with whom we have "face time," the virtual personages on-screen have identities and invite our emotions. . . . Sometimes we evaluate them as physical beings and moral agents. Often we find them desirable, or enviable, or in some other way they evoke the sentiments, the liking, irritation, or boredom, that flesh-and-blood individuals evoke. . . . They take up ritual places as heroes, leaders, scapegoats, magical figures, to be admired, envied, loved, or hated; to *matter*.[3]

The options that our more contemporary communication technologies give us for sharing images is mind boggling. Their impact is also profound. New images can be generated and sent synchronically.

An image—still or moving—lingers in our memory much longer than written or spoken words. The stronger the emotional tug of an image, the longer it will stay with us.

In today's world, image is rapidly replacing the value of the written word. The versatility of social networks exponentially increased the power of images and the ways in which we use them, share them, or exploit them. There is a very real possibility that image-driven perceptions will eventually dominate our communication patterns.

THE POET LAUREATE

The Bible is mostly story. It was, of course, originally communicated in a written format. Though Scripture's narratives happened in faraway places and ancient

---

1 Marshall McLuhan and Quentin Fiore, *The Medium is the Massage: An Inventory of Effects* (New York: Bantam Books, 1967), 14.

2 Todd Gitlin, *Media Unlimited: How the Torrent of Images and Sounds Overwhelms Our Lives*, rev. ed. (New York: Henry Holt and Company, 2002), 20.

3 Gitlin, *Media*, 21.

Though Scripture's narratives happened in faraway places and ancient times, God's story continues to shape the culture of His people.

times, God's story continues to shape the culture of His people. The people who came to life in Bible stories we learned as children are not only historical figures, they are also metaphors for our lives. In Job's suffering, we contemplate our own suffering. In Jacob's wrestling match with God, we see ourselves wrestling with God. In Thomas's doubt, we are forced to examine our own weak and wavering faith. With Peter's confession, we measure our own confidence in Christ and His promises.

The Bible is also poetry. The poetry of Scripture is every bit as important, and as inspired, as its prose. David wrote, "My heart overflows with a pleasing theme; I address my verses to the king; my tongue is like the pen of a ready scribe" (Psalm 45:1). The psalmist's "pleasing theme" is nothing less than God's plan to redeem us. The Twenty-Third Psalm or Mary's splendid Magnificat have the power to transport us to the very gates of heaven. And because all Bible poetry is Spirit-breathed, faith is the blessed miracle that results from being exposed to such divinely expressed truths.

God's Word is an inspired mix of prose and poetry—historical fact integrated with verses that lift us to soaring heights. Its author is the poet laureate of eternity.

There is one literary dynamic that helps make the prose and poetry of the Bible resonate with the earthy now of this present life. We will call this remarkable device the Bible's "word pictures."

The richly inviting word pictures that appear throughout Scripture help bind all the strands and topics of Scripture together into a unified whole. Also inspired, these simple metaphors resonate with everyone. They are commonly understood references to the ordinary stuff that is part of our everyday experience: trees that give life, provide the raw resources that can be used to build arks, yield fruit, or serve as instruments of torture and death. Temples with living souls as their building materials. Stones that sing. Blood that cleanses sinful hearts. Water that quenches the human thirst for freedom from condemnation. Cups that overflow with grace. Fishing nets that catch people. Winds that gather and disperse people. A city's beacon that draws people together, where glory never stops growing. A piece of cloth or animal skins that cloak immoral living or cover human imperfection. This is imagery designed for informing the human spirit: clay pots, mustard seeds, a whispered voice, bloody doorframes, a wisp of smoke, a stairway to heaven, a fiery chariot, a lamb, a child, a star, blood, family, wind, tents, smoke, water, fruit, a wedding banquet, and bread. Without them, the story of God's love would still covey the same simple, heart-changing truth. But that truth would remain flat, like a two-dimensional Mercator map distorts the spherical shape of our planet.

God's Word is an inspired mix of prose and poetry—historical fact integrated with verses that lift us to soaring heights. Its author is the poet laureate of eternity.

The story of Christ's resurrection is essentially recorded in Scripture as prose. The empirical facts of His victory over death is human history of unparalleled significance. Each Gospel narrative lays out the facts of an event that occurred in real time and in a real place. The Gospel writers speak in a definitive voice, making tangible the story's characters, plot, setting, tension, and climax. Like a headline, all four Gospels echo the same hope-filled narrative: "Christ Conquers Death!"

Take a closer look. There are details in the Bible's telling of the resurrection event worth further exploration. The garden, for example. Or mention of a brilliant light. And what about Pilate's official seal? These details haven't merely been inserted as props to make the story work. They are much more important than that. Each pictured detail adds another dimension to the narrative.

Life on our planet had its origin in a garden. Adam and Eve were driven from a garden of perfect communion with their Creator. When Jesus prayed to His heavenly Father, asking that His cup of suffering be removed, it happened in a garden. This was no accident. The garden imagery of Easter morning connects us to other parts of Scripture, and we are driven to ask why God chose a garden as the setting for this event.

Pilate's seal on the tomb was more than window dressing. Rome symbolized earthly kingdoms. The hunk of wax that Pilate ordered to seal Jesus' tomb highlights the tension between the human kingdoms and God's transcendent kingdom. Yes, Pilate did hold Jesus' life in the governing power of his human hands. But only the almighty God of life and death has the power to reverse the curse of death and restore vitality to a lifeless body. The same imagery shows up in John's Revelation, where the Lamb is the only worthy candidate capable of opening the seven wax seals to reveal the great mysteries of God's triumph over His enemies as encouragement for those of us left to carry out the heavenly commission of sharing Jesus with a hopelessly lost kingdom still bound in time, space, and change.

The bright light of the resurrection story is hardly coincidental. Light filled the sky on the night of Jesus' birth, shining brightly to capture the attention of the sleepy shepherds. Luke calls this special light the "glory of the Lord"—*kebod YHWH* in Hebrew (2:9). It was an Old Testament reference to God's phys-

In faith, we believe what the Bible tells us, because we have virtually no natural experience in God's eternal kingdom.

ical presence among His people. Every Jew knew the significance of this Hebrew expression. The children of Israel saw the *kebod YHWH* flashing brightly at the top of Mount Sinai. God's people witnessed His visual glory in the pillar of fire that guarded their camp at night and in the column of cloud that guided their travels by day. Moses saw the Lord's glory in the train of His holy robes as I AM passed by the rock that Moses was hiding behind. John's Gospel begins by connecting divine light with life and the living Word. Light was the first thing created. Christ was there, creating it. The light that confronted Saul on the way to Damascus emanated from Jesus Himself. And Jesus introduced us to a new facet of our Christian identity when He declared, "You are the light of the world" (Matthew 5:14). These word pictures convey divine truth. They enrich our perspective and add impact. They will linger in our memory forever.

A TWO-KINGDOM WORLDVIEW

There are challenges in living, as all believers do, with one foot planted in the human realm of time, space, and change and the other foot planted in God's spiritual kingdom. For one thing, we can't see God. Nor can we touch Him, smell Him, hear Him, or taste Him. In scientific terms, God is an anomaly. In faith, we believe what the Bible tells us, because we have virtually no natural experience in God's eternal kingdom. The human Jesus struggled with this same challenge. It is one reason why word pictures appealed so much to Him as a teacher. At best, we can only hope to imagine things that are beyond our experience, even when our mind's eye is operating with a sanctified 20/20 vision.

But imagination is able only to sate our thirst for a little more understanding and set our curiosity afire. Faith, not imagination, extends our spiritual view beyond the limitations of time and space. Faith helps us rise above the obstacle of sin and the limitations of being human. Faith allows us to have a foretaste of God's infinite and eternal kingdom. While we are left blithering over the conundrum of how faith accomplishes this, faith opens our eyes to, and unites us with, the eternal work of God. This is where the Bible's narratives and word pictures converge and go to work. Constructed from the stuff of ordinary human experience, God's Word has the power to transport us beyond our human limitations to a whole new vista of spiritual understanding and a kingdom that is truly not of this world—a kingdom of limitless power, incomprehensible wisdom, absolute truth, endless peace, infinite grace, unbounded joy, pure goodness, unqualified hope, uncompromising justice, endless love, transcendent glory, and life everlasting.

Abstract Bible concepts are difficult to grasp, which is what makes these Bible word pictures all but indispensable. They serve as bridges that can transport us from the known of our earthly time-space-change experience to the heart of our loving God.

Faith allows us to have a foretaste of God's infinite and eternal kingdom.

Into this changing world, God sends his unchanging Gospel, connecting words to images and images to hearts. There, in hostile human hearts, God's Spirit brings about real and lasting change. Death becomes life. Darkness turns to light. Enmity is transformed into friendship. Hatred is overcome by love. Wherever God's narrative of Christ and His cross is heard, it touches hearts and faith flourishes. The Good News of salvation in Christ Jesus changes everything.

The Bible's picture language is a perfect fit for our contemporary setting. It is a perfect tool to foster the spiritual growing that you and the other members of your family need for your souls. God's pictured themes tell a story about the only reality on our planet that has ever mattered.

Today's young people are not readers in the traditional sense, but they are interested in story, and they are fascinated with the vocabulary of image and symbol. They are quickly drawn to the image-enriched story of God's enduring love for His fallen creatures. The poetry, prose, and the many word pictures of Scripture will enrich your family's spiritual life.[4] Your family's faith in God's enduring promises will become strong, and your relationship with Him, and with one another, will grow.

THE CLUETRAIN MANIFESTO

Do you recall when you first heard about the Internet? If you are over thirty, you might remember how you were introduced to this powerful, new communication tool. For many of us it happened in the early nineties. Back then, people referred to it as "www" or "the Web." The Internet came with its own peculiar vocabulary: email, download, attachments, hyperlinks, chats and chatrooms, webpages, surfing the Web, blogging, instant messaging. It was like learning a foreign language.

While most of us saw the Internet's potential for staying in touch with distant friends, people in marketing were drooling over the Internet's potential for selling record-breaking quantities of whatever they were pitching. For a few years, the dot-com stocks associated with this exciting new technology went through the

4 See Matthew 7:7.

roof. But by the mid-nineties, everyone was asking the same question: Why can't we make piles of money using the Internet? It wasn't as though they had not been trying. Whatever they were doing just wasn't working. No one seemed to have the answer. Eventually, the big investors began to lose their confidence in the online market. Finally, the bubble burst, and a lot of people lost a lot of money.

In 1998, four marketing gurus were commissioned to consider the elephant in cyberspace. Their think tank generated a series of ninety-five theses. A book about their work was published year or so later with the unusual title *The Cluetrain Manifesto*. Today, the book is considered a classic.

None of this would have mattered, except that one of the four marketing gurus had a special interest in the history of marketplaces. He decided to compare the ancient model of a marketplace with the way marketing business was being conducted on the Internet. He discovered that people moved about freely from vendor to vendor in the ancient marketplaces. Folks could inquire about a product's origin. They compared prices and talked with other shoppers about each vendor's integrity and the quality of his product. Only then was it possible to attach value to the products that were for sale. At the same time, those who came daily to the ancient marketplaces used the opportunity to catch up on the latest news. Ideas were exchanged, stories shared, opinions debated, current news was passed on from one person to another. The place was alive with human interaction. People were largely interested in many of the same things. All the elbow-rubbing was a positive communal activity. It brought people together, giving them the sense that they were all in the same boat—and, at the same time, all part of something bigger than their own piddling lives.

When the marketing expert compared the ancient model to the mass-marketing practices of the last hundred years, he realized that the modern marketplace was lacking élan. The dynamic was not very interactive either. In fact, nearly all of the technology-based marketplaces of the last century were overwhelmingly one-dimensional. The customer did not have a voice. You can't talk back to a radio. TVs don't respond to our questions. Mass mailings can show pictures of happy customers, but they don't actually fill in details about the products they are promoting. All the give-and-take had disappeared. Gone were the opportunities to ask questions, compare prices, or evaluate the product's quality or the vendor's integrity. Additionally, in the modern marketplace the ability to connect with other people in their community had been removed.

When the Internet arrived on the scene in the early 1990s, everyone assumed it was just another new technology, tailor made for the mass-marketing practices of the last hundred years. Business went on as usual, using the one-dimensional model that had worked so well in the past with radio, television, and mass mailings. But the Internet was not that kind of medium.

When *Cluetrain* was released in 2000, much of what the four gurus had to say sounded like old news. Almost no one paid attention to their ninety-five theses. But a handful of words appearing in chapter 4 resonated: "Markets are nothing more than conversations. . . . Our only hope is to talk. Starting now."[5]

To put this into a historical perspective: In 2003, LinkedIn was the first of the social networks to appear on the Internet. It was quickly followed by Facebook (2004), YouTube (2005), and Twitter (2006). The correlation between this initial observation in *Cluetrain* and the advent of social networks is obvious.

Today, social networking has changed the way we think and behave. In one sense, we are all captive to it. It has become an important part of our culture. It has also become a part of us, a natural part of our day-to-day lives.

In the spring of 2012, Felicia Wu Song provided a perspective that challenged Christians to take the time and expend the energy to, at the very least, examine the implications that technology has spread before us.

> As digital technology has progressively become embedded and institutionalized into the everyday practices of public and private life, the need to understand how these practices are subtly shifting the boundaries of our imagination and reframing, or reworking our notions of friendship and relationships becomes greater. . . . To do this we need to get behind the frames of thinking we are given culturally and see our technologies anew. As philosopher Kwame Anthony Appiah exhorts, "In the real world, the act of framing and describing the situation and, thus, determining there's a decision to be made, is a moral task. It is often THE moral task. Learning how to recognize what is and isn't an option is part of our ethical development." These questions, I believe, are particularly acute for people of Christian conviction, who believe that human beings, being created in the image of God, are essentially relational creatures."[6]

---

5 Rick Levine et al., *The Cluetrain Manifesto: The End of Business as Usual* (New York: Basic Books, 2000), 76.

6 Felicia Wu Song, "Facebook, Friendship, and the Search for Real Community," videographed lecture, Beimfohr Lecture series, sponsored by Chesterton House at Cornell University, April 10, 2012, accessed January 7, 2017, www.cornell.edu/video/facebook-friendship-and-the-search-for-real-community.

Kwame Anthony Appiah is a contemporary British philosopher. He has taught at Yale, Cornell, Duke, Harvard, and New York Universities. He is globally respected for raising ethical questions regarding the collision of technology and cultural/social values. (See appiah.net.)

I didn't hear about *Cluetrain* until I attended a communications symposium in St. Louis in 2005. In my profession, a lot of time is spent attending seminars, symposiums, workshops, and conventions. (Some of my fondest daydreams have occurred during seminars, symposiums, workshops, and conventions.) For a presentation to leave a lasting impression on me, it has to have the impact of a runaway freight train hitting a wall head-on at 190 miles an hour. When I heard those six words, I bolt upright, unable to speak, and thoroughly engaged in thought. Some of the people sitting near me later confessed to having had a similar experience. During the break, the room was abuzz with talk: "The marketplace is a conversation." Everyone was engaged, inspired, enthralled by what they had just heard.

Then it washed over me like a giant tsunami! For all of my adult life, communication had been my thing. I was passionate about it. Why had I not heard this before? And why, for heaven's sake, didn't my church know about it?

The wheels were still turning that night as I lay awake in my motel bed. I thought of Jesus' ministry on earth. I was astounded at how much of His work had occurred in the marketplaces of His day. This is how He reached out to sinners. He worked the marketplaces, meeting with strangers, asking them questions that would begin conversations. He brought His disciples along to learn His techniques. They watched as He warned the Jewish leaders, healed the lame, befriended the lonely, confronted the wealthy, encouraged the poor, admonished the proud, forgave the guilt-ridden, and corrected the confused. They saw how He listened to people and talked with those who were dying to hear His message.

Jesus reaches out to us in the same way—in a conversation. Do you remember sitting on a grandparent's knee, eating at a dinner table, hanging out on the front porch, or having a serious conversation with your best friend? Jesus talk just happens. Why haven't we encouraged one another to engage Him in a personal conversation? Is it possible the church has settled for letting the market come to us? Are we afraid of the wrestling matches that await our engagement when we share ourselves with others? Have we been so immersed in mass-marketing our message when people are hungry for a personal conversation to help them wrestle with the questions that trouble them? And why haven't we invited Jesus into the marketplaces of our own homes, where meaningful conversations about things that really matter are such a rare thing these days? Have we become complacent about sharing the truth that opens up eternity for the people we call family?

As for me and my house, we will serve the Lord.

—Joshua 24:15

CHAPTER 13

THIRTY, SIXTY, A HUNDREDFOLD

I AM is shaping us, forming our new man in Christ, preparing us to live as His people in an ever-changing and often hostile world.

The search for a moral mankind does not begin or end in the human heart, but in the heart of a loving and righteous God, who left His kingdom's throne to become our human brother. In Him alone is the moral good that all mankind is seeking. But in knowing His infinite goodness, Christians are unique. God's Spirit gives us the courage to humbly distinguish ourselves from the unbelieving world—to, in effect, be the common, ordinary, everyday utensils whom God Himself has set apart for His service. The lens of faith that we peer through to understand ourselves and the world in which we live is different. Our convictions are different. Our way of life, what motivates us, our spiritual outlook, how we make our decisions, how we spend our time and money, how we dream about the future or remember the past, how we approach our work, our recreation, and our rest, or how we treat the people around us—everything about us is different. Sometimes, we rebel. Our faith does not always season our conversations with the savory voice of a saint or shine brightly into some dark den of unbelief. We occasionally resent our "different" status. Our culture teaches us that blending into the crowd is the best way to survive. Besides, living like the rest of the world—sharing its one-kingdom values and social principles—is so much easier.

Being a Christian is not for spiritual sissies. We are still children, striving to attain our full moral maturity, and still adults, wondering how God's Spirit will work the miracle in us to become spiritually childlike once again. I AM is shaping us, forming our new man in Christ, preparing us to live as His people in an ever-changing and often hostile world. He is training us to be His agents of change, difference-makers, blessing-seekers, people-lovers, and cross-bearers—all roles that demand a large measure of help from an all-powerful God with an endless array of resources at His disposal. How good, then, to know that God's people reside on the Mountain of the One Who Provides! He is God, we are not.

In his book *We Believe—Therefore We Speak*, David Valleskey reflects on the radical transformation that takes place in the believer's heart, while expanding the horizons of our own identity to include four additional facets of who we are. Valleskey writes:

> Christians do not have to suffer from an identity crisis. They know who they are. Christians are "a chosen race, a royal priesthood, a holy nation, a people belonging to God." Nor must Christians be uncertain regarding their purpose. These four titles, "chosen people," "royal priesthood," "holy nation," "a people belonging to God," R. C. H. Lenski reminds us, are not "static but dynamic." Christians have become something for a purpose. Peter clearly states that purpose: "that you may declare the praises of him who called you out of darkness into his wonderful light." (1 Peter 2:9 [NIV]). That is what God looked for from Israel, "the people I formed for myself," he says, "that they may proclaim my praise" (Isaiah 43:21 [NIV]). Now he looks for praise from his new people.[1]

THE SOWER AND THE SEED

Glory giving is a difficult notion to conceptualize. Does it happen only in worship settings or when we pray or sing songs of praise? Can glory be given to God by a schoolboy playing with his toy trucks? How does someone proclaim His glory when that individual identifies as an athlete, a mom, a dad, a scholar, a soldier, a dentist, a nurse, a student, a retiree, an entrepreneur, a drama instructor, a retail clerk, a police officer, a factory worker, a farmer, a politician, a computer analyst, a felon, or a sinner like you or me? How would Jesus describe this glory-giving function as it plays out in our lives?

---

1 David J. Valleskey, *We Believe—Therefore We Speak: The Theology and Practice of Evangelism* (Milwaukee: Northwestern Publishing House, 1995), 147–48. Quotation from R. C. H. Lenski, *The Interpretation of the Epistles of St. Peter, St. John and St. Jude* (Columbus, OH: Wartburg Press, 1945), 102.

The question takes us full circle to the place where we began our conversation. The biblical answer begins to take shape as early as the creation narrative in Genesis 1, where we learn about the first living things on earth.

> And God said, "Let the earth sprout vegetation, plants yielding seed, and fruit trees bearing fruit in which is their seed, each according to its kind, on the earth." And it was so. The earth brought forth vegetation, plants yielding seed according to their own kinds, and trees bearing fruit in which is their seed, each according to its kind. And God saw that it was good. (Genesis 1:11–12)

Before birds, fish, animals, or human creatures filled the garden, God made sure that vegetation was available to feed them. Once that fact had been established, Moses quickly moved on to fill in yet another critical detail of the creation event: the miracle of reproduction.

Without the ability to procreate, life on our planet would not be sustainable. Seeds—for future generations of flowers, grasses, trees, but also fish, birds, insects, animals, and human seeds—are critical components in the ongoing process of regeneration.[2] Understanding the important function that reproduction plays in the story of life on our planet will help us conceptualize spiritual reproduction, which is the main theme of Jesus' parable of the sower.[3]

On this day, the crowd was so large that Jesus waded out to a small boat bobbing at anchor. He clambered into the boat and began to teach, using His favorite teaching method, the parable.

> A sower went out to sow. And as he sowed, some seeds fell along the path, and the birds came and devoured them. Other seeds fell on rocky ground, where they did not have much soil, and immediately they sprang up, since they had no depth of soil, but when the sun rose they were scorched. And since they had no root, they withered away. Other seeds fell among thorns, and the thorns grew up and

---

2 The Jews of antiquity remained steadfast in celebrating their family history, and the history of God's people, with succeeding generations. They seem to have understood the significance of the generational concept better than we do. Today, the emphasis on generational history has all but disappeared. Most of us do not think generationally beyond four generations. God inspired His writers to promote the idea of generational history through a variety of religious observances. Begetting a family always included a responsibility to pass the narrative of God's abundant grace and undeterred faithfulness on to their children and grandchildren. The Book of Esther, and especially Esther 9:23–28, stresses this point with great clarity.

3 Robert Farrar Capon, *Kingdom, Grace, Judgment: Paradox, Outrage, and Vindication in the Parables of Jesus* (Grand Rapids: Eerdmans, 2002), 57. Capon calls this parable "the great watershed of all Jesus' parables."

> choked them. Other seeds fell on good soil and produced grain, some a hundredfold, some sixty, some thirty. He who has ears, let him hear. (Matthew 13:3–9)

When Jesus finished telling the story, one can only imagine how folks looked at each other in complete puzzlement. They had no clue to what He was trying to teach them. Perhaps the closing line made more sense than the parable itself; was the point something about ears and hearing?

Meaningful conversations are hard to come by these days. Most of us are isolated by our own interests, introverted by our own problems, and insulated by our own insecurities.[4] When we are so stuck on ourselves, we alienate those who are the most important people in our lives. In the current cultural climate, honest dialogue about the issues that separate people from one another has given way to political correctness, hyperbole, and manipulation. In the silence of our throw-away exchanges, many of us find ourselves becoming more or less irrelevant.

Jesus has a solution for irrelevance: "He who has ears to hear, let him hear" (Matthew 11:15). God's people need to listen. We need to learn how to listen to one another to understand where others are hurting or in need. We need to hear Jesus pour His heart out to us in words of divine love. When we stop listening to God, we stop seeking His presence in our lives. And separation from God's love is a definition of hell.

At this point, Matthew interrupts with a brief, but instructive, sidebar (11:10–17). Apparently, during the break, Jesus' followers came to Him privately to ask why He used parables to teach the people. The Master explained that He used parables to reveal truths about His kingdom that would strengthen their faith. For those individuals, whose hearts had already been hardened in unbelief, parables hid the same saving truths, making it impossible for God's judgment to be reversed.[5]

Then Matthew returned to Jesus' parable and its interpretation.

> When anyone hears the word of the kingdom and does not understand it, the evil one comes and snatches away what has been sown

---

4 In our era, some of the isolation may be due, in part, to a phenomenon known as compartmentalizing, which makes it possible to hold contradictory convictions without experiencing deep emotional disorientation. The moral implications of this phenomenon are profoundly troubling.

5 James F. Pope, *When Christ Walked among Us: The Messiah's Life and Ministry* (Milwaukee: Northwestern Publishing House, 2012), 57. Pope writes, "When God commissioned the prophet Isaiah to carry out his work seven centuries before the birth of Jesus, he informed the prophet that he would be delivering a message to the Israelites and many of them would reject it. . . . But still Isaiah kept delivering God's message to those people. . . . Isaiah's experience foreshadowed Jesus' ministry. Jesus' parables strengthened faith in those who already trusted in him as their Savior, while on the other hand, they hardened people who rejected him even more in their unbelief." (See Isaiah 6:9–10.)

> in his heart. This is what was sown along the path. As for what was sown on rocky ground, this is the one who hears the word and immediately receives it with joy, yet he has no root in himself, but endures for a while, and when tribulation or persecution arises on account of the word, immediately he falls away. As for what was sown among thorns, this is the one who hears the word, but the cares of the world and the deceitfulness of riches choke the word, and it proves unfruitful. As for what was sown on good soil, this is the one who hears the word and understands it. He indeed bears fruit and yields, in one case a hundredfold, in another sixty, and in another thirty. (Matthew 13:18–23)

With most of His parable lessons, Jesus left His congregation chewing on their own interpretation. He knew that healthy dialogue is an effective way to make people wrestle with real issues and practical applications. In this case, however, the Master carefully doubled back to help His hearers understand the parable's meaning. Yet, even with His outstanding explanation in hand, we are left with some unanswered questions to ponder. Who, for example, is the sower? A case could be made that the sower is human and the parable is a homocentric narrative about the work we do as members of Jesus' Great Commission Team. It is true that God's people sow the seeds of the Gospel. And all Christians know that we work for the Great Commissioner. But when the sower resembles ourselves, the narrative tends to take on a subtle spin that reflects our self-centered worldview. The parable's interpretation then is slightly tarnished, and Jesus' message takes on the timbre of a "Get Busy" speech, rather like JFK's famous "Ask not what your country can do for you" inauguration address. But Jesus' purpose here is not so much to motivate as it is to teach us a fundamental truth about, of all things, reproductive life in His spiritual kingdom.

In the most common interpretation, the Sower is God. He is casting seed here and there, more or less at random.[6] The seed is His living Word—Law and Gospel.[7] He is spreading that seed in four separate sections of the field. Each location produces its own unique results.

Some seed falls on a hardened footpath. Exposed, these seeds have no chance of surviving. The birds quickly swoop in and eat every last seed.

6 See John 3:5–8.

7 For a brief study of biblical word pictures describing the Holy Spirit's work of planting, cultivating, and harvesting, consider Genesis 2:8; Psalm 1:3; Luke 13:6; James 1:21; 1 Corinthians 3:5–9; Matthew 9:37; John 4:35; Revelation 14:14–16.

The Teacher is picturing folks who fail to appreciate what He has done for them. They may respect Him, but they do not grasp the new life they could rightfully claim for themselves because of His work. Nor do they make any effort to learn about His kingdom. Instead, their hearts become hardened to the Good News of salvation. Some are not aware that they are rejecting Christ's life-changing message. Others know, but have made a conscious decision to go it alone. The devil makes short shrift of such individuals, luring them into false narratives that replace God's grace with human imagination or personal accomplishment.[8]

Another potential insight is that the ever-efficient Sower allows none of His precious seed go to waste. At His behest, nature puts the hungry birds to flight, causing them to redeposit the seeds they've just eaten in other locations that might be more productive.[9]

Some seed fell in a rocky place. This soil, if one can call it that, has no nutrients. Worse, the drainage is terrible. Still, a few seeds manage to sprout in the cracks between the rocks. Their hopeful beginning is short lived. With no minerals, moisture, or biological compounds to renew the soil's fertility, the little seedlings shrivel up in the hot sun and blow away in the wind.

The rocky soil symbolizes people who are familiar with Jesus and His message. These people received the Gospel with enthusiasm, but they have failed to grow in their faith. They may have received biblical instruction, but they did nothing to be regularly reassured by God's promises from His living Word.[10] Before long, their souls starve from spiritual malnutrition. In direct disobedience to God's instructions, these folks did the unthinkable. By failing to daily rehearse the Bible's song of divine grace, they soon forgot what great things God had done for them.

Some of the precious seed was also sown in a section of the field that had deteriorated into a briar patch. These seeds also sprout. But the tiny shoots have their life choked away as the larger, more aggressive weeds block the sunlight and leech all the nutrients and moisture hidden in the soil.

The weedy field symbolizes people who hear God's Word and initially take its saving message to heart. But worldly matters—material concerns, social climbing, abuses, careers, addictions, the love of wealth, family troubles, arguments with the

---

8 G. Jerome Albrecht and Michael J. Albrecht, *Matthew,* The People's Bible (Milwaukee: Northwestern Publishing House, 1996), 195. "The devil calls God a liar, and many believe his lies and go with him to eternal destruction. God wanted to save them and invited them into his kingdom, but they simply declined his gracious invitation. . . . God does not drive or drag anyone into his kingdom by force. Christ died for everybody and redeemed the whole world, but those who despise his salvation and reject him rightfully remain in Satan's kingdom for time and for eternity."

9 See Isaiah 55:11.

10 For a brief Bible study on the power and purpose for God's Word, consider 2 Timothy 3:15; Hebrews 4:12; Psalm 119:103, 105, 114, 116; 1 Corinthians 2:4–5; Colossians 3:16; James 1:22.

church, hardships, false gods, and sinful habits cause them to lose their spiritual focus. These seeds also perish.

It would be hard to miss Jesus' cautionary tone in this part of the parable as He lays out the realities of unbelief. At base level, the sin of unbelief leads to death and eternal destruction. This portion of the parable teaches us: "A faith that is small and weak saves a person for heaven just as well as a strong, heroic faith saves. But we must not be satisfied with a weak faith because it can so easily be snuffed out. We rather want to put on the whole armor of God, so that we are fully protected against anything that might threaten to destroy our faith."[11]

At this point in the narrative, there is a radical change in the Rabbi's tone. An air of jubilance and celebration suddenly lifts Jesus' hearers as He announces that the Sower has also spread Gospel seed on a field of good soil. The harvest from this field will multiply the Sower's original investment many times over. The net return could be as much as thirty, sixty, or a hundredfold. Yet, the fact that any seed has actually borne fruit is what makes the Sower so happy. The God of immeasurable grace and mercy is not in the business of counting; He is in the business of celebrating His success.[12]

God's people identify with the fourth field. We understand that we are not "good" soil because of something we've done. We became "good" by virtue of the righteous life Jesus lived for us. We, therefore, identify as His children, His flock of lambs and sheep, His Bride, His Body, His branches, His broken pots, ambassadors, beacons of light, brothers and sisters, royal priests, salt, living letters, chosen people, temples made of human hearts, and now, as His fields of regenerated good soil. Everything we are flows directly from who He is. The seed of the Gospel sprouts and grows, and God provides every spiritual resource we need to bear fruit. The harvest will be used in the service of His kingdom.[13]

We became "good" by virtue of the righteous life Jesus lived for us.

This is the good life—the distinguished, reproductive life of everyone who knows and worships the name of Jesus. As God's created, redeemed, and sanctified people, we are always becoming more like Him, replicas of the divine image embedded in the soul of humankind when time began. The remedial formula for

11 Albrecht and Albrecht, *Matthew*, 195–96. (See Ephesians 6:10–18.)

12 See Isaiah 55:12.

13 Small Catechism, explanation of the Second Article. Martin Luther wrote, "[Jesus] redeemed me, a lost and condemned person, purchased and won me from all sins, from death, and from the power of the devil. . . . That I may be His own and live under Him in His kingdom and serve Him in everlasting righteousness, innocence, and blessedness, just as He is risen from the dead, lives and reigns to all eternity. This is most certainly true."

Christian character now reads more like $C = I + P^x$, or Performance increases exponentially.

THE GODLY FAMILY

We have opportunities every day to bear fruit in our interactions with the people who are part of our everyday comings and goings. Our homes are marketplaces for daily conversations. In some households, the conversations that center around Jesus and His Word just happen. And they probably happen quite often. Maybe, if anyone is counting, they happen daily. Other families have to work at it. Still others are paralyzed by a lack of self-confidence or impeded by their family's spiritual dysfunction. The spiritual communication in these homes is compromised and tentative. No matter how hard they try, or how much they long for it, the Jesus conversations just never occur. Such families need our loving attention. They need evangelical assistance to remove whatever impasse is hindering their growth. Their faith life needs to be rescued from spiritual lethargy. They desperately need spiritual intervention.

The home is a natural place to cultivate a healthy environment for sharing Jesus with one another.

The home is a natural place to cultivate a healthy environment for sharing Jesus with one another. Lawrence Richards provides an apt description of the day-to-day activity in a spiritually healthy family.

> Scripture must be communicated as a lived and livable reality! Its truths must be communicated by those who have integrated them into their personalities and who, in the shared experiences of life, talk the Word and words of God with their children. The critical location for Bible teaching is not the classroom but rather the household; the walk, the sitting together on the porch, the snuggling into the warmth of bed, the joy of rising to a new day. It is in life itself, where Bible truths are to have meaning for us as whole persons, that our communications must center.[14]

For some of us, this description sounds like a holy platitude. It isn't. As a matter of record, such families actually do exist, though not one is perfect. They read and discuss Bible stories with their children, share their faith in Jesus with one another, seek God's forgiveness, make godly choices, and pray together. Some of their faith life at home is organized in a formal way, to accommodate schedules and ob-

14 Lawrence O. Richards, *A Theology of Christian Education* (Grand Rapids: Zondervan, 1980), 193 .

ligations. Most of their religious conversation, however, is spontaneous. They are familiar enough with their Bibles to be able to seek God's guidance and direction or find the strength to share the burdens that other members of their family might be carrying. They are never afraid to engage the Stranger—to seek answers to life's most difficult questions. They communicate with one another with a loving attitude that mirrors Jesus' own selfless love and compassion. On a regular basis, they join other members of His spiritual Body to worship their God and remember His profound goodness.

We might be shocked to learn just how few of today's Christian households are actually engaged in some kind of daily spiritual activity at home.

Such families are becoming rare. We might be shocked to learn just how few of today's Christian households are actually engaged in some kind of daily spiritual activity at home. We might be even more shocked to learn that a fair number of folks who have been called into God's service as career church leaders have forgotten that godly families actively seek God's presence in their daily lives.

Some of us are just lazy. Many of us are distracted by the details of our human kingdoms. Some of us are ashamed of our past. Some of us are wrestling with sins that have become a persistent thorn in our present. Some are afraid of being exposed as biblically illiterate. Many do not have a healthy spiritual model to draw upon from their own childhood. Some marriages struggle with diverse religious worldviews. The whole family is often engaged in a silent conspiracy to avoid spiritual conversations to maintain peace and stability in the home. Perhaps no one has bothered to tell them that the peace and stability they may be achieving for their household comes at the risk of losing the peace and stability of their eternal future. Other families develop a cavalier attitude about their faith. They may have been ignoring their need for daily sustenance and renewal for years.

If your household is any one of the above, use this conversation as an opportunity to give the matter your prayerful thought. Talk about it with other Christians who have overcome a shallow spiritual lifestyle. Do something to change the status quo. There's no time like the present to begin. God isn't measuring how much you produce; He is waiting to join you in celebrating the harvest in your field.

A FINAL WORD FOR CHURCH LEADERS

We began our conversation expressing concern about living as God's people in a culture that daily grows more hostile to our faith. This conversation needs to continue and grow. The subject is urgent because the spiritual life of future generations is in jeopardy. The painful truth, however, is that the threat posed by our anti-Christian culture pales in comparison to the threat of our own complacency. Too many of God's people have not been bearing fruit in our own backyards. Spiritual neglect is morally indefensible.

Christian converts living in first-century Rome wanted to be excused for their sluggish spiritual performance. The social pressures of living in a pagan culture were, no doubt, stifling and sometimes dangerous. New converts had good reasons to sit on the sidelines and excuse themselves from being salt and light. They were poorly prepared for teaching and ill-trained for communicating. They had little confidence in their Bible knowledge. Most of them had never been exposed to Old Testament traditions. They needed time to get up to speed. Some may have been concerned about a bewildered or hostile pagan spouse. Their excuses remind us of a reluctant Moses, engaged in a private conversation with a chatty, flaming shrub. These are the last people on earth one might imagine God choosing for such a challenging assignment. In spite of all this, Paul seems almost duty bound to not excuse them. Choosing his words carefully, the apostle writes straight from the heart: "I myself am satisfied about you, my brothers, that you yourselves are full of goodness, filled with all knowledge and able to instruct one another" (Romans 15:14).

The apostle knew that these folks were not Bible scholars. But they were good fields of fertile soil. Their faith in Jesus gave them the kind of spiritual knowledge that made them competent to instruct one another about God's heavenly garden and a Savior who welcomes sinners into His enchanted kingdom.

The same is true for God's people living in our era. Many still shrink from studying Scripture because they have never learned how to approach God's Word. The church needs to provide more opportunities for lay members to develop hands-on Bible study skills and attitudes. They need to overcome their lack of self-confidence in their own understanding of Bible history or in the basic teachings of God's Word.

Members also hesitate to share Jesus with others because they have never done anything like that before. Well, they won't get a chance to try it unless church leaders insist on constructing learning models that train their lay members to function at home as their family's spiritual leaders. Thankfully, some pastors are beginning to recognize that their first task is to give their members opportunities to learn by doing and not merely by telling them what they should do.

Godly leaders also have to lead by example. We need to be more open to recognizing those precious teachable moments when important topics appear out of the blue. Teaching is often more effective when it happens spontaneously. We need to organize our own family's prayer life in a way that gives everyone a chance to express their own thoughts to God. More important—and this is the critical part we so often forget—everyone needs to be given opportunities to see how God answers their prayers. We need to invite the worshipful praise of each family member in the same way we invite members into God's house, so that no one ever forgets the blessings of holding a lifetime membership in God's enchanted kingdom. And, more than any other thing, we need to lead—yes, *lead*—our families to the cross with the same energy and enthusiasm reserved for our members, who know exactly where to go with their guilt.[15]

Godly leaders also have to lead by example.

Joshua's role was to prepare the children of Israel for entering their new homeland. Before crossing the border, he addressed them as their spiritual leader, pointing out that God was always with them. He recalled that their success in battle was possible only because God had been faithful to His promises. Then Joshua redirected their thoughts to the moment everyone had been waiting for—their grand entrance into the land flowing with milk and honey, a new genesis for the children of Israel.

> Now therefore fear the LORD and serve Him in sincerity and in faithfulness. Put away the gods that your fathers served beyond the River and in Egypt, and serve the LORD. And if it is evil in your eyes to serve the LORD, choose this day whom you will serve, whether the gods your fathers served in the region beyond the River, or the gods of the Amorites in whose land you dwell. But as for me and my house, we will serve the LORD. (Joshua 24:14–15)

The highest priority of a good leader is to equip, train, and inspire others to lead. Leadership in the church community is no exception. Follow Joshua's model by emulating all three elements of successful leadership with your own living example.

In real life, the metaphorical journey into God's promised land is long and difficult. It is that for the members of our families, just as it is for the members of our congregations. The goal is in plain sight to motivate us and get us moving in the right direction. We do not travel alone; Immanuel is with us. We never lose contact, even when we are off the grid; the God of Jacob is always in touch. We know who we are; we are God's children—His lost, last, least, and the vulnerable little ones. We know why we are here: to bear fruit. We are certain of our desti-

15 See Romans 5:1–11.

nation; our eternal home is with God in heaven and then the new creation. All that is left in the time He provides is to kneel in humble awe and whisper a silent prayer: *Come, Lord Jesus. Come into our hearts and rule forever. And make of us what You will. Amen.*

Soli Deo Gloria

From the Author

It's called "The Great Shema." The expression comes from a Hebrew word that means "hear," or perhaps "listen up." The term perfectly captures the absoluteness of the moral authority found in Deuteronomy 6:4: "Hear, O Israel: The Lord our God, the Lord is one . . ." What follows the intense call to listen up is God's own "How-To Approach to Living the Moral Life." This is God speaking to us. He is keeping His solemn promise to provide the right words for Moses to use as he introduces the Ten Commandments to the children of Israel with authority and grace. Practicing Jews still keep the tradition of reciting the Shema every morning and every night before falling asleep.

I first learned about the Shema when I was perhaps two or three years old, but not from Moses. Nor, for that matter, from Jewish parents. My folks were staunch Lutherans. In one of my earliest childhood memories, I am sitting in the lap of either my father or mother, listening to my favorite Bible stories being read to me from a big Bible story book as I contemplate with delight the colorful pictures. One story stirred my imagination so profoundly that I begged to have someone read it to me every night. The story was about a young boy named Samuel. Though he lived more than three thousand years before I was born, Samuel and I seemed to have something in common (1 Samuel 1–4).

Samuel lived with an old priest named Eli. At the request of Samuel's mother, Eli was training Samuel for a lifetime of service to God's people. As the plot thickens, we learn that God had already chosen Samuel as His spokesman. The narrative tells us that the Lord came to Samuel one night as he lay in bed: "Samuel . . . Samuel!" Samuel mistakenly thought old Eli had called him. But each time Samuel went to attend to Eli's needs, the old man told Samuel he had not called and sent the youngster back to bed.

When this happened a third time, Eli realized the voice Samuel was hearing was the Lord's. The old priest told Samuel that if he heard the voice again, he was to respond by saying, "Speak, LORD, for Your servant is listening." This was the part of the story I loved most. I admired Samuel's intense yearning to hear the Lord speak to him. I wanted to be just like him.

A few years later, as a young Christian educator, I found myself teaching that same Bible story to young teens. I still loved the narrative, but quickly noted that my perspective had changed. Instead of seeing myself in young Samuel's sandals, I now discovered that the character of old Eli was better suited to my adult worldview. As a young father, I saw the flawed old man wrestling with issues that many parents, like me, were facing every day. I knew from the storyline that Eli would die soon. Though only in my twenties, I was beginning to see myself as fragile and flawed. On the other hand, my instinct, like old Eli's, was to do the right thing—to speak to the young Samuels in my classroom and at home with the moral authority vested in me by God Himself. My message was inspired: *Listen up! God has something important to tell you.*

Years later, and well into my career, I bumped into the Shema again as the choir director in my local congregation. I had discovered a moving piece of music based on Isaiah's vision in chapter 6. My choir was excited to showcase the musical work in their next concert.

In Isaiah's vision, we witness the prophet entering the majestic throne room of the high and exalted King of heaven and earth. Through Isaiah's eyes, we get to see what he saw. Resplendent heavenly beings flitted about, serving the Lord and glorifying His name. Then, just as we are beginning to soak up all the glory of the throne room, Isaiah realizes he shouldn't be there in the presence of the holy God. "Woe is me!" he cries (v. 5). Isaiah is morally blemished by his own wretched character. But in Isaiah's moment of despair, the Lord sends an angel to cauterize his sinful lips with white-hot coals, indicating he has been cleansed of all his leprous unrighteousness. God is preparing Isaiah for a special task. "Go, and say to this people: 'Keep on hearing, but do not understand; keep on seeing, but do not perceive.' Make the heart of this people dull, and their ears heavy, and blind their eyes; lest they see with their eyes, and hear with their ears, and understand with their hearts, and turn and be healed" (vv. 9–10). God's people had not responded to the moral authority of their almighty God. They had not listened. They had violated and abused God's Shema. His patience has run its course. He is about to harden the hearts of His own people. Isaiah's mission was to proclaim this distressing prophecy among the people, calling them to repent and change from their godless ways.

It wasn't until I began to think about writing this book that a pattern started to emerge. It happened when I first noticed that the Old Testament ended by recalling the Shema: "Remember the law of my servant Moses, the statutes and rules that I commanded him at Horeb for all Israel. Behold, I will send you Elijah the prophet before the great and awesome day of the LORD comes. And he will turn the hearts of fathers to their children and the hearts of children to their fathers, lest I come and strike the land with a decree of utter destruction" (Malachi 4:4–6). Now I could see the Bible as a continuum of divine pleas for God's people to remember Him and His promise of grace. The Shema's call to remember and teach was just as prevalent in the New Testament as it was for the Israelites of old. (See Luke 2:52; Matthew 19:13–15; Ephesians 6:1–4; or 2 Timothy 1:5.) Today, the Gospel reverberates throughout a world still rotting in sin and desperate for a solution to its moral decay. For God's family of believers, the Shema holds its ground, reminding God's people to remember Him daily.

The book you hold vibrates with the urgency of all three Old-Testament voices. Little Samuel's stirring response to God's call still fills the night. So does the trembling utterance of a broken, old priest named Eli, as he gently encourages us to let God speak. But it is the jarring words of warning and judgment, falling from the prophet's lips, that need to resonate most as we struggle to produce fruit in a culture hostile to our faith. Again, the question is, are you listening? Do you hear it? Shhh! A Stranger stalks our camp. He comes like the wind, with invisible stealth. Relentless, He engages us. Then, once more, we find ourselves locked in a life-and-death struggle, and we are humbled. Every muscle strains to demand His loving blessing. Fight on, dear Christian. Jesus has already won the victory over sin, death, and hell for you. God will provide whatever resources you need. You know who He is. Contend with Him through the darkest night. Acknowledge the pain. You cannot lose. When the battle has ended, and the blessing is yours, cherish your new identity and return to your home to stoke the embers of faith in the family hearth. There, together with your nearest and dearest, cherish the love, the peace, and the transcendent joy of life forever in His eternal embrace.

KJK

APPENDIX A

Discussion Guide

CHAPTER 1: HIGH-LEVEL CONVERSATIONS

Themes: *change; conversation; courage.*

1. Define *character* in your own words.
2. What is the most glaring difference between the worldviews of the two thieves?

   Why is it important to distinguish between the character of unbelievers and Christians?
3. If you could change one aspect of the relationships in your home, what would it be?
4. List obstacles and barriers to meaningful conversations between parents and their children.
5. Why will we need an extra measure of courage to engage in this conversation?

   How will God's people acquire the kind of courage these issues demand?

CHAPTER 2: THE BLESSING

Themes: *worldview; character formation; life's purpose; identity; performance.*

1. Define *worldview.*
2. How does the fact that God created humankind "in Our image" impact you or your life?

   How does the fact that God gave humankind dominion to rule over the earth impact your life?
3. Why is it important to know the origin of human character?
4. What is the significance of the first four words of Genesis 1:28 ("And God blessed them")?
5. Evaluate the following statement: "When we fail to thank God for blessings, we begin to take His love for granted."
6. What is your strategy for training your child(ren) to look for God's blessings every day?
7. How does the formula for human character, C = I + P, help you understand yourself?

CHAPTER 3: HOW CHARACTER IS FORMED

Themes: *character; Christian (godly) character; family; community; learning; conscience.*

1. Make a list of Bible truths that parents should emphasize daily when their child is young.
2. Does your child love you? How do you know? Do you love your child? How do you know?

   Why is it important for parents to daily remind their children they are loved unconditionally?
3. During the testing phase, what are some challenges that Christian parents have to endure?
4. Evaluate the following statement: "I send my child to a Christian school because I want him to be a good person."

5. Evaluate the following statement: "If we do not teach our children to love Jesus, the world will teach them not to."

6. Why is it important for Christian parents to grow in faith and biblical understanding?

7. What encouragement does Romans 15:14 offer to parents regarding their family's faith life?

CHAPTER 4: A SIREN'S SONG

Themes: *cultural purging; secular humanism; transcendency; two kingdoms; moral authority.*

1. What signs do you see that suggest the moral worldview of our culture is deteriorating?

2. Does knowing the tipping point was reached around 1970 help you better understand the culture?

3. Read Romans 13:10–14. Why should Christians pay attention to our changing times?

4. Are people tired of the evolution versus creation debate? Should we continue to discuss it?

6. How does one train a child to be discerning when it comes to evaluating new ideas?

7. What evidence do you see to support C. S. Lewis when he said, "Man is on the bench and God is in the dock"? How does the breakdown of authority affect life in this world?

CHAPTER 5: A MODEL FOR ALL TIME

Themes: *narcissism; God's house; the mask; wrestling with God; divine testing; Israel's child.*

1. Are there ways in which we might despise God's blessings and barter them away? Explain.

2. How are the masks we wear to cover sin connected to our conscience?

3. What does the expression "house of God" mean to you?

4. What elements of Jacob's good fight with God resonate with you? Explain.
5. What does God mean when He invites us to test Him? What does He not mean?
6. What insights can we gain when we see Jesus as the "One Who Wrestles with God"?

CHAPTER 6: BUILT ON THE ROCK

Themes: *foundations; a name for ourselves; theocracy; New Testament church as a culture.*

1. In your opinion, who is telling the story that is shaping our culture today? Explain.
2. Why are we typically more concerned about what others think about us than what God thinks?
3. How did confusing the people's language at Babel show God's abiding love for mankind?
4. Why is it important for Christians to study the historical narratives of Scripture? (See John 5:39.)
5. How does God make His 24/7 presence known in your life?
6. What are the most significant differences between Babel's culture and Israel's culture?
7. What are the distinguishing characteristics of the Christian Church on earth?

CHAPTER 7: YEAST BEAST

Themes: *legalism; training children to be Pharisees and Sadducees.*

1. Do Christians celebrate Passover today? Explain.
2. Explain how the metaphor of yeastless bread relates to God's grace.
3. How does the toxic yeast of the Pharisees and Sadducees find its way into our hearts today?

4. Which kind of yeast (Sadducees or Pharisees) influences our church more today? Explain.

5. Do you agree that the gospel most Americans trust in is "following your dreams and being so good that God will make all of your dreams come true"? Explain.

CHAPTER 8: BECOMING

Themes: *faith; trust; humility.*

1. Why did God give Adam the task of naming the animals? (See Genesis 1:26; 2:19–20.)

2. How does faith grow to become strong and resilient?

3. What lesson was Jesus teaching when He had a young child brought into the room?

4. If humility is a problem in our national culture, is it also a problem in the church? Explain.

5. How was our spiritual condition at birth different from Jesus' spiritual condition at birth? How does the Bible explain this difference?

6. How does the formula C = I + P help you see how God's people serve God's eternal plan?

CHAPTER 9: A TWO-KINGDOM LENS

Themes: *life, as seen through a two-kingdom lens; knowing by faith; eschatological worldview.*

1. How can parents help their child learn *how* to learn? Explain and/or discuss.

2. What thoughts would you offer to someone who wants to learn more about God and His love?

3. What kind of activities do we engage in every day as stewards and caretakers of God's creation? How has God personally equipped you for this task?

4. How do you daily engage in the task of being good stewards of your spiritual blessings?

How do you care for the souls of the members of your dear family?

5. Make a list of ways in which God blesses us through change.

6. Break down the meaning of each phrase in 1 Corinthians 13:8–12. Why are the last seven words (of v. 12) so significant?

CHAPTER 10: TWO KINDS OF RIGHTEOUSNESS

Themes: *the faith/love connection;* I AM, *and you are a branch, a pot, salt, and light.*

1. How do you picture your relationship with God?

   a. How do you picture your relationships with your fellow human beings?

   b. How does your relationship with God influence your relationships with people?

2. Evaluate the following statement: "Faith is not the end of the story that God has prepared for us."

3. What has Jesus has saved us *from*? What has Jesus saved us *for*? Explain the distinction.

4. Describe your identity and performance as:

   a. a *branch* that is attached to Jesus the Vine;

   b. God's *clay pot*;

   c. *the salt of the earth*;

   d. *the light of the world.*

CHAPTER 11: A MORAL EDUCATION

Themes: *morality in American education; Enlightenment; deism; psychological humanism; habitus; informed parents; life's purpose.*

1. Why should all parents know the underlying ethic of the school their child attends?

2. List blessings that result from *religious tolerance.* Are there any unfavorable or challenging aspects of religious tolerance? Explain.

3. How should Christian parents address unbiblical ethical positions when they are taught in public schools?

4. Are the foundations of our American culture wearing thin? Explain.

5. Make a list of effective ways for Christian parents to influence the faith life of their children.

6. What kind of spiritual activity would you like to introduce in the daily life of your family?

CHAPTER 12: IN THE MEDIA TORRENT

Themes: *word pictures in Scripture; imagination; the marketplace of conversation.*

1. Who is telling the story that is shaping our culture today?

2. In what significant ways have the various media and digital technologies changed our culture? In what ways have these technologies changed you or your family?

3. Are there any topics of conversation that are taboo in your home? Explain why they are taboo.

4. Do your children know their moral boundaries? Give some positive or negative examples.

5. How would you begin to evaluate the spiritual health of your own household?

6. What reasons do members of a Christian family have for sharing their faith with one another?

7. What conversations should Christians have about living in a culture that is hostile to our faith?

CHAPTER 13: THIRTY, SIXTY, A HUNDREDFOLD

Themes: *bearing fruit; the godly family; commitment and accountability.*

1. Evaluate the following statement: "The greatest joy of following Jesus is the joy of bearing fruit for His kingdom."

2. Describe what you think bearing fruit for God's kingdom looks like in your life.

3. In concrete terms, what does "bearing fruit for Jesus' kingdom" mean? What does it have to do with you or your family?

4. What points in this book did you need to hear?

5. What questions have been raised by this book that deserve further thought and discussion?

APPENDIX B

Biblical Character

This is a working document. It is incomplete and open to additions, deletions, and corrections. Your suggestions can be posted at embracingchristiancharacter .com. The purpose of this list is to highlight biblical virtues and values that Scripture presents as integral to a person of godly character. Some traits have been grouped together to avoid redundancy.

Accepting: *James 2:1, 8–9; 3:17; Hebrews 13:1–2; Romans 14:1–4; 15:7; 1 Timothy 5:21.*

Accountable: *Hebrews 4:13; Romans 3:19; 14:12; Matthew 12:36; 1 Peter 4:5; Ezekiel 18:20.*

Charitable, Benevolent, Hospitable, Friendly, Loving, Generous: *1 Peter 1:22; 4:8; Galatians 6:1; James 4:12; Ecclesiastes 11:1; Isaiah 58:6–8; Matthew 10:42; 25:33–40; 1 Corinthians 13:2–8, 13; 16:14; Ephesians 5:1; Philippians 1:9–11.*

Chaste, Modest, Pure in Heart: *Proverbs 5:20; 1 Thessalonians 4:3–5; Deuteronomy 5:18; Philippians 4:8; Matthew 5:8.*

Cheerful: *Proverbs 15:13; 17:22.*

Civic-minded: *Titus 3:1–2; 1 Peter 2:13–17; 2 Samuel 10:12; Romans 13:7; Matthew 22:21; Nehemiah 4:21.*

Compassionate, Humane, Selfless: *2 Chronicles 28:15; Luke 10:33–34; Galatians 6:2; Hebrews 13:3; Isaiah 58:7; Ephesians 4:22–24; Matthew 15:32; Psalm 82:3.*

Content, Serene: *1 Timothy 6:6, 8; Hebrews 13:5; Philippians 4:11; Colossians 3:15.*

Courageous, Encouraging: *Deuteronomy 31:6; Ezra 10:4; Daniel 6:10; Psalm 118:6; Ephesians 6:10–20; 1 Thessalonians 5:11; Romans 15:1–2; 1 Corinthians 14:12; 16:15; Hebrews 3:6; Acts 4:13.*

Courteous, Kind: *Colossians 4:5–6; Romans 12:10.*

Dedicated, Devoted: *Exodus 32:29; Proverbs 23:26; Romans 10:1; 12:1; Deuteronomy 6:5; Psalm 119:2; John 4:34; 9:4; Acts 4:20; 1 Corinthians 9:16, 22; Philippians 3:13; 2 Timothy 2:15; Colossians 1:29.*

Ethic, Work/Rest: *Ecclesiastes 5:19; 9:10; 1 Corinthians 15:10; 2 Thessalonians 3:10; 1 Thessalonians 5:12; John 9:4.*

Faithful, Loyal: *Matthew 25:21; 1 Corinthians 1:8–9; 4:17; Revelation 2:10; 19:11; 1 Chronicles 29:18; 1 Kings 8:56; Psalm 36:5; Hebrews 6:18; 10:23; 2 Thessalonians 3:3.*

Forgiving, Patient, Merciful, Long-suffering: *Colossians 3:13; Ephesians 4:2; Isaiah 48:9; Luke 23:34; Matthew 5:7, 23–24; 6:12.*

Frugal, Good Steward: *Genesis 41:36; Proverbs 12:27; 21:20; John 6:12; 16:1-9; Matthew 6:33; Psalm 24:1.*

Fruitfulness: *Luke 8:39; John 15:5, 16; Romans 7:4; Philippians 1:11; Colossians 1:10; Matthew 13:8; Galatians 5:22–23; James 3:17; Proverbs 1:3.*

Gentle, Meek: *1 Thessalonians 2:7; Luke 6:29; Galatians 5:23; 1 Peter 3:4; Psalm 37:11; Matthew 5:5; 11:29; Isaiah 53:7; 2 Corinthians 10:1.*

Honest, Having Integrity, Honorable, Sincerity, Trustworthy, Loving Truth: *Ephesians 4:25; 2 Kings 12:15; Nehemiah 13:14; Daniel 6:4; 1 Corinthians 4:2; Leviticus 19:35–36; Romans 13:8.*

Humble: *Matthew 5:3; 7:3–5; 11:29; 18:1–4; 2 Corinthians 10:1–5; 12:9–10; Isaiah 53:7; 1 Peter 5:5–6; Ephesians 2:8–9; Mark 9:14–29; James 4:6–10; Genesis 11:1–9.*

Joyful: *Isaiah 12:3; 61:10; Psalms 16:11; 126:2; 1 Peter 1:8; John 16:20, 24; Romans 14:17; Hosea 2:15; Luke 10:20.*

Just, Fair-minded: *Deuteronomy 16:20; Proverbs 21:3; Isaiah 56:1.*

Obedient: *Proverbs 10:8; Hebrews 12:1–2; Matthew 10:24; 1 Peter 1:14, 22; James 4:17; Leviticus 5:17; Psalm 119:2.*

Peace-loving: *Proverbs 14:30; 17:1; 25:21–22; Matthew 5:9, 38–44; 1 Peter 3:9; John 18:11; James 3:18; Psalms 34:14; 133:1; Ephesians 4:26; 2 Corinthians 5:19–20; 1 Thessalonians 4:11.*

Persevering, Industrious: *Proverbs 10:4; 13:4; Romans 12:11; 1 Corinthians 4:11–16.*

Prudent, Wise, Discerning, Thoughtful: *James 3:17; Hosea 14:9; Proverbs 6:8; 9:12; 14:15; 15:15; 22:3.*

Responsible, Conscientious, Diligent: *2 Peter 3:14; Proverbs 18:9; 1 Corinthians 4:2; 1 Timothy 6:20; 1 Peter 4:10.*

Reverent, Respectful: *Exodus 3:5; Psalms 33:8; 89:7; Habakkuk 2:20; Leviticus 19:30; John 2:16; 1 Thessalonians 5:12–13; Deuteronomy 10:12; Ecclesiastes 12:13; 1 Peter 2:17; Joshua 24:14; Isaiah 8:13; Matthew 10:28.*

Self-controlled, Temperate, Sober: *James 1:26; 1 Peter 1:13; 2 Peter 1:5–7; Titus 2:2.*

Teachable, Seeking Understanding: *Matthew 5:6; 13:23; Hebrews 4:12–13; Proverbs 7:2; 9:9; 18:15; 19:20; James 1:21; 2 Timothy 3:16; 2 Thessalonians 2:15; Psalm 119:2; Jeremiah 29:13; Luke 2:49; Revelation 3:19; 2 Peter 1:5.*

Thankful, Grateful: *Colossians 3:15; Philippians 1:3–6; 2 Samuel 9:1; Psalm 9:11; Hebrews 13:15.*

Tolerant: *Matthew 9:10; 13:24–30, 36–43; Mark 9:38.*

Trusting, Hopeful: *Luke 1:37; 1 Peter 1:3–9; Romans 5:4; 8:28; 10:9; Psalms 4:5; 31:6; 37:5; 118:8; John 5:24; 20:31; Matthew 8:1–4, 5–13; Proverbs 3:5; Isaiah 12:2; 26:4; 50:10.*

Zealous: *John 2:17; Isaiah 61:2; 2 Timothy 1:3; Numbers 25:13; Galatians 4:18.*

APPENDIX C

Two Different Worldviews

This is a working document. It is incomplete and open to suggestions for additions, deletions, and corrections. Post your suggestions to the website embracingchristiancharacter.com. The purpose for this document is to compare the tenets of two worldviews that serve as the ethical foundations of secular education and Christian education. Secular humanism is generally agreed upon as the foundation for most, if not all, secular (public) schools in America. Many private schools also subscribe to secular humanism as the basis for their ethic. The other worldview referenced here is the underlying ethic of Christian education. Christian education embraces the Bible as the headwaters for this ethic. Most, if not all, Lutheran schools use Scripture as the ethical foundation for their educational model.

1. How Are the Models of Secular Education and Christian Education Similar?

- God uses both models to bless people with learning that will serve them in this life.
- Both models generally have student learning as their primary mission and function.
- Both models operate under the direction of trained people who are also sinners.
- Both models teach skills, knowledge, and attitudes that help learners live in a sinful world.

- Both models share a common interest and understanding of pedagogy.
- Both models represent communities (cultures) that claim to be based on a moral ethic.
- Both models exist in a pluralistic culture of ideas, traditions, history, artistic expression, and so on.
- Both models deal with a similar set of natural and man-made obstacles to learning.

2. How Are the Supporting Worldviews of These Two Unique Educational Models Different?

Ethical Topic	*Secular Humanism Model*	*Christian Education Model*
Accountability	Individual is accountable to a self-determined moral code that is interpreted by legal and social norms.	All humankind is ultimately accountable to God's will as it is expressed in His Word, the Bible.
Advancement	Humankind is the measure of all progress.	God blesses humankind with the intellectual gifts and natural resources to advance human civilization according to God's will.
Adversity	Face adversity with perseverance and inner strength.	We wrestle with God for all of our blessings, including the strength to deal with adversity.
Authority	Rule of law as opposed to rule by tyranny. The individual is accountable to the authority of the land. Social mores are taught as an authoritative ethic.	God has authority over all things, which He exercises with perfect justice and gracious compassion. God shares limited authority with individuals whom He has placed into roles of authority.
Benevolence	Be selfless by giving back to the community. Benevolence is seen as payback to the community.	Give glory to God by showing your love for others as a reflection of Christ's love for you.
Change	Events are cause-neutral. Humankind is capable of managing change and manipulating outcomes.	A changeless God created an environment of constant change for humankind. God uses change to bring about His good and loving will on behalf of His people. God calls upon His people to serve as agents of change.

Ethical Topic	*Secular Humanism Model*	*Christian Education Model*
Character	Character is largely understood as being self-generated, but culturally and socially influenced.	God changes sinful hearts through the power of His Word and the Sacraments of Baptism and the Lord's Supper to empower God's people to live according to God's commands in response to His unbounded forgiveness and love.
Conflict Resolution	Rule of law and the tools of mediation, negotiation, and arbitration are reliable ways to resolve conflict. One can find internal peace through various forms of intervention and therapy.	Biblical reconciliation through forgiveness and absolution ends conflict by healing broken hearts and restoring damaged relationships to their original state. Strategic tools such as mediation, arbitration, and negotiation are gifts that God has given to humankind to maintain order and restore peace. These gifts do not, however, lead to fully restored relationships.
Coping	Find the strength to cope within yourself.	Find strength, comfort, encouragement, and hope for coping from God by reading His Word and trusting His promises.
Enemies	Human tyranny is understood as humankind's greatest enemy.	The enemies of our soul are sin, death, and the devil's power to undermine our faith in Jesus.
Ethic, Work/Rest	A balanced cycle of work and rest can support and replenish the physical and emotional aspects of human beings.	Work and rest are blessings from God. In love, He gives us these gifts to help us maintain our physical and emotional health. Our future life in heaven includes God's promise to provide eternal rest from our labors on earth.
Faith	Trust human intelligence to succeed in life.	Trust in God's loving promises to uphold you now and forever.
(The) Future	Hope resides in humankind's ability to prevail in every challenge. Learning model is focused exclusively on life in this world of earthly kingdoms. Life after death is uncertain and open to debate.	Our hope is grounded in the divine intervention of God's great redemptive work of resolving humankind's problem with sin and guilt. God's promise of eternal life is for all who believe in Jesus.

Ethical Topic	*Secular Humanism Model*	*Christian Education Model*
God	Humankind imagines god in terms of a human image.	"I AM WHO I AM": Creator, Redeemer, and Sanctifier—three individual persons, yet one God, who reveals Himself to humankind through His inspired Word, the Bible.
Guilt and Conscience	Guilt harms the child's psyche. Therapy aims at neutralizing the negative effects of a damaged psyche that results from guilt.	A guilty conscience indicates that we have sinned and need to repent and seek God's mercy and forgiveness.
Heaven	A mythological place or state of mind. Public schools are bound by law to refrain from teaching children about heaven or how to get there.	Eternal life with God in heaven is for all who believe in His promises. Heaven is real. It is a spiritual "place" where there is no sadness, sin, or suffering. (In this book, we have also used the word *enchanted* to emphasize the profound wonder that heaven belongs to all who believe in Jesus.)
Hell	A mythological place or frame of mind reserved for bad people who deserve to be punished with a painful existence that lasts forever.	A spiritual reality of endless hatred, self-loathing, and suffering, where there is no relationship with God or access to His love. Unbelievers will languish forever in hell for their sin of unbelief.
History	A record over time of human achievement.	Scripture is the divinely inspired record of God's promises made to humankind and kept over the course of time and in eternity.
Jesus Christ	A great teacher who lived about two thousand years ago; a good, wise man, but not the Son of God or the Savior from sin. Public schools are bound by law not to teach that Jesus is our Savior or the Son of God.	Son of God, sent by His Father to live a perfect moral life and die as our substitute to save us from punishment for our immoral lives.
Knowledge	Human knowledge has the power to resolve all of humankind's most serious issues and improve life on our planet.	The human mind is a gift from God. It has great potential for improving life on earth. Spiritual knowledge is also a gift from God. It holds the key to eternal life in heaven with God. Spiritual knowledge can be grasped only by faith in God's promises, which are found only in God's Word, the Bible.

Ethical Topic	*Secular Humanism Model*	*Christian Education Model*
Marriage	Cultural norms define the parameters for marriage.	God ordained marriage for one man and one woman. Divorce is reserved for situations in which one spouse has been unfaithful to the promise that was made between husband and wife.
Mortality	Death is part of the repeating circle of life. Public schools are not permitted to teach what happens to the individual after death.	The wages of sin is death. God judges sin. The punishment we deserve is everlasting separation from God. The penalty has been paid for with the blood of God's own sacrificial offering of His Son's life. For the believer, death is the threshold to eternal life in heaven with God and a cause for celebration. Jesus' resurrection from the grave guarantees that we, too, will rise victorious over death.
Motivation	Fear of the law; communal reward for civic works.	Christians are motivated by love for their Savior to do good works on behalf of others as bearing good fruit for God's kingdom on earth.
Natural Condition	Children are born into this life uncorrupted and innocent of any wrongdoing. People are naturally good.	All people are born into this life corrupted by sinful impulses and are, therefore, also naturally and spiritually blind, dead, and enemies of God. This natural sinful state is called original sin.
Origin of Life	All life is the result of an evolutionary process.	God called all life into being by divine fiat.
Prayer	Reassuring self-talk. Praying to one god is as good as praying to another.	God hears the prayers of believers and responds to their prayers in their own best interest. God does not hear the prayers of unbelievers.
Providence	Hard work usually makes good things happen. Good fortune can also play a role in achieving our earthly goals.	All blessings come from a gracious God, who promises to provide for all our needs and keeps that promise according to His divine wisdom and will.

Ethical Topic	*Secular Humanism Model*	*Christian Education Model*
Purpose	One's purpose in life is largely self-determined and usually self-serving. Humanitarian endeavors are encouraged and praised for having been done for the good of society.	The life purpose of God's people was determined in eternity to give glory to God. We are commissioned by Jesus to serve Him by bearing fruit in the form of good works. Sharing the Gospel message is the epitome of fruit-bearing in God's kingdom.
Resource	Protect and preserve the earth's resources in the best interest of future generations.	God's creation is a blessing for all humankind to enjoy and use wisely. God has given to humankind the role of being good stewards of His creation.
Sanctity of Life	Mixed messages. Respect all forms of life. Cultural norms determine society's moral position on abortion and euthanasia.	All life is a blessing from God. Human life is precious. God forbids humans to take another human life except in cases of self-defense, in war, or at the hands of the government for committing a heinous felony.
Satan (the devil)	A mythological boogeyman.	Satan is real, powerful, deceptive—a fallen angel. He seeks to lead souls away from their saving faith in Jesus' sure promises.
Sin	We all make mistakes. These mistakes can include actions and behaviors that hurt other people. Some mistakes are unacceptable to the point that they deserve communal punishment or reprimand. We are all ethically accountable to our community. By law, accountability to God's Law cannot be taught in public schools.	Sin damns. We are tainted by sin and cannot save ourselves from its damning effects, which is everlasting death. Even though He was innocent of all sin, Jesus willingly died the death that all sinners deserve in order to save all members of the human race from eternal damnation.
Suicide	A poor choice because things might improve. A terrible waste of a human life.	A sin against the Fifth Commandment, suicide ends a person's time of grace, when only the Giver of life has that right.

Ethical Topic	*Secular Humanism Model*	*Christian Education Model*
Truth	Ethical or moral truth is subjective. Empirical truth (scientific truth) is as close to pure truth as one can get. Truth that is derived from the rule of law or popular opinion is also commonly understood as a determining form of social truth.	Divine truth is absolute, immutable, and authoritative. Such truth can be found only in God's Word. Human versions of truth are not absolute, are subject to change, and can be understood as authoritative only insofar as our limited human reason determines.
Will	Largely self-determined.	God's will is sovereign, and His will is always achieved. God has given to humankind a free will to make choices and decisions. The will of natural sinful humankind does not align with God's will. A Christian's sanctified will (the new man in Christ) desires to please God, and with God's help can bear the fruit of good works. The unbeliever's will is hostile to God's will and fights against it.

Bibliography

Albrecht, G. Jerome, and Michael J. Albrecht. *Matthew*, The People's Bible. Milwaukee: Northwestern Publishing House, 1996.

Barna, George. *Revolutionary Parenting: Raising Your Kids to Become Spiritual Champions*. Carol Stream, IL: Tyndale House, 2007.

Becker, Siegbert W. *The Foolishness of God: The Place of Reason in the Theology of Martin Luther.* Milwaukee: Northwestern Publishing House, 1982.

Bennethum, D. Michael. *Listen! God Is Calling: Luther Speaks of Vocation, Faith, and Work.* Minneapolis: Augsburg Fortress, 2003.

Biermann, Joel D. *A Case for Character: Towards a Lutheran Virtue Ethics.* Minneapolis: Fortress, 2014.

Bosch, David J. *Believing in the Future: Toward a Missiology of Western Culture.* Harrisburg, PA: Trinity Press International, 1995.

Boyd, Gregory A. *The Myth of a Christian Nation: How the Quest for Political Power Is Destroying the Church.* Grand Rapids: Zondervan, 2005.

Brooks, David. *The Road to Character.* New York: Random House, 2015.

Capon, Robert Farrar. *Kingdom, Grace, Judgment: Paradox, Outrage, and Vindication in the Parables of Jesus.* Grand Rapids: Eerdmans, 2002.

Cherney, Ken. "Hidden in Plain Sight: Luther's Doctrine of Vocation." *Wisconsin Lutheran Quarterly* 98. No. 4. (2001).

Concordia Self-Study Bible, The. St. Louis: Concordia Publishing House, 1986.

Ehlke, Roland Cap. *Like a Pelting Rain: The Making of the Modern Mind.* Abridged version. Milwaukee: EhlkeWorks, 2013.

Franzmann, Werner H. *New Testament*, vol. 1. Bible History Commentary. WELS Board for Parish Education. Milwaukee: Northwestern Publishing House, 1989.

———. *Old Testament*, Bible History Commentary. WELS Board for Parish Education. Milwaukee: Northwestern Publishing House, 1980.

Galstad, Martin. *Findings: Explorations in Christian Life and Learning*. Second expanded edition. Milwaukee: Wisconsin Lutheran College Press, 2008.

Gitlin, Todd. *Media Unlimited: How the Torrent of Images and Sounds Overwhelms Our Lives.* Revised edition. New York: Henry Holt and Company, 2002.

Gopnik, Alison. *The Philosophical Baby: What Children's Minds Tell Us about Truth, Love, and the Meaning of Life.* London: The Bodley Head; Random House, 2009.

Hauerwas, Stanley. *The Peaceable Kingdom: A Primer in Christian Ethics.* Notre Dame, IN: University of Notre Dame Press, 1983.

Hunter, James Davison. *The Death of Character: Moral Education in an Age without Good or Evil.* New York: Basic Books, 2000.

Jeske, John C. *Genesis,* The People's Bible. Milwaukee: Northwestern Publishing House, 2001.

Johnson, Barrett. "How to Raise a Pagan Kid in a Christian Home," INFO for Families. November 13, 2013, accessed May 7, 2016, http://www.infoforfamilies.com/blog/2013/11/13/how-to-raise-a-pagan-kid-in-a-christian-home#.UuBHYP16i-w=.

Kolb, Robert, and Charles P. Arand. *The Genius of Luther's Theology: A Wittenberg Way of Thinking for the Contemporary Church.* Grand Rapids: Baker Academic, a division of Baker Publishing Group, 2008.

Kratz, Kenneth R. *The Word Speaks: 365 Devotions Based on the Sayings of Jesus.* Milwaukee: Northwestern Publishing House, 2011.

Kretzmann, Paul E. *Old Testament,* vol. 1. Popular Commentary of the Bible. St. Louis: Concordia Publishing House, 1923.

Lange, Lyle W. *God So Loved the World: A Study of Christian Doctrine.* Milwaukee: Northwestern Publishing House, 2005.

Lawrenz, Carl J., and John C. Jeske. *A Commentary on Genesis 1–11.* Milwaukee: Northwestern Publishing House, 2004.

Levine, Rick, Christopher Locke, Doc Searles, and David Weinberger. *The Cluetrain Manifesto: The End of Business as Usual.* Cambridge, MA: Perseus Publishing, 2000.

Linder, Douglas O. "State v. John Scopes ('The Monkey Trial'): An Account." Famous Trials. Accessed May 29, 2017. http://www.famous-trials.com/scopesmonkey/2127-home.

Lewis, C. S. *God in the Dock: Essays on Theology and Ethics.* Edited by Walter Hooper. Grand Rapids: Eerdmans, 1970.

———. *A Year with C. S. Lewis: Daily Readings from His Classic Works.* Edited by Patricia S. Klein. New York: HarperCollins, 2003.

Luther, Martin. *Luther's Small Catechism with Explanation.* St. Louis: Concordia Publishing House, 2017.

Lutheran Book of Worship. Minneapolis: Augsburg Fortress; St. Louis: Concordia Publishing House, 1978.

McCarraher, Eugene. "We Have Never Been Disenchanted." *The Hedgehog Review* 17. No. 3 (2015).

McLuhan, Marshall, and Quentin Fiore. *The Medium is the Massage: An Inventory of Effects.* New York: Bantam Books, 1967.

Montgomery, John Warwick. *The Law Above the Law: Why the Law Needs Biblical Foundations; How Legal Thought Supports Christian Truth.* Irvine, California: NRP, 2015.

Platt, Suzy, ed. *Respectfully Quoted: A Dictionary of Quotations.* New York: Barnes and Noble Books, 1993.

Pope, James F. *When Christ Walked among Us: The Messiah's Life and Ministry.* Milwaukee: Northwestern Publishing House, 2012.

Reuter, David L. *Teaching the Faith at Home: What Does This Mean? How Is This Done*? St. Louis: Concordia Publishing House, 2016.

Richards, Lawrence O. *A Theology of Christian Education.* Grand Rapids: Zondervan, 1980.

Rousseau, Jean-Jacques. *Emile* or *On Education.* Translated by Allan Bloom. New York: Basic Books, 1979.

Smith, James K. A. *How (Not) to Be Secular: Reading Charles Taylor*. Grand Rapids: Eerdmans, 2014.

Sorabji, Richard. *Moral Conscience through the Ages: Fifth Century BCE to the Present.* Chicago: University of Chicago Press, 2014.

Sunshine, Glenn S. *Why You Think the Way You Do: The Story of Western Worldviews from Rome to Home.* Grand Rapids: Zondervan, 2009.

Taylor, Charles. *A Secular Age.* Cambridge, MA; London: Harvard University Press, 2007.

Valleskey, David J. *We Believe—Therefore We Speak: The Theology and Practice of Evangelism.* Milwaukee: Northwestern Publishing House, 1995.

Walsh, David, Kristin Parker, and Monica Walsh. *Dr. Dave's Cyberhood: Making Media Choices That Create a Healthy Electronic Environment for Your Kids.* New York: Simon and Schuster, 2001.

Walther, C. F. W. *God's No and God's Yes: The Proper Distinction between Law and Gospel.* Condensed by Walter C. Pieper. St. Louis: Concordia Publishing House, 1973.

Wu Song, Felicia. "Facebook, Friendship, and the Search for Real Community." Videographed lecture. Beimfohr Lecture series. Sponsored by Chesterton House at Cornell University. April 10, 2012. Accessed December 18, 2016. www.cornell.edu/video/facebook-friendship-and-the-search-for-real-community.